Minding the Store

Minding the Store

A BIG STORY ABOUT
A SMALL BUSINESS

by Julie Gaines

Illustrated by Ben Lenovitz

ALGONQUIN BOOKS OF CHAPEL HILL 2018

Published by
Algonquin Books of Chapel Hill
Post Office Box 2225
Chapel Hill, North Carolina 27515-2225

a division of
Workman Publishing
225 Varick Street
New York, New York 10014

Printed in China.
Published simultaneously in Canada by Thomas Allen & Son Limited.
Design and color by Rose Wong

Library of Congress Cataloging-in-Publication Data

Names: Gaines, Julie, author. | Lenovitz, Ben, illustrator.
Title: Minding the store : a big story about a small business /
by Julie Gaines ; illustrated by Ben Lenovitz.
Description: First edition. | Chapel Hill, North Carolina :
Algonquin Books of Chapel Hill, 2018.
Identifiers: LCCN 2018011663 | ISBN 9781616206628 (hardcover : alk. paper)
Subjects: LCSH: Fishs Eddy (Firm) | Tableware. | New business
enterprises— Management. | Stores, Retail— Management. | Family-owned
business enterprises— Management. | Entrepreneurship.
Classification: LCC HD9971.5.T324 .F574 2018 | DDC 338.7/64270973— dc23
LC record available at https://lccn.loc.gov/2018011663

10 9 8 7 6 5 4 3 2 1
First Edition

To Vivian and Valerie, and mothers everywhere.

CONTENTS

Introduction   1

1. Road to Fishs Eddy   5

2. For Rent   13

3. Doing Dishes   29

4. Customer Service in the Early Years   41

5. Family Business   55

6. Road Scholars   63

7. In the Black   75

8. Half-Baked   91

9. Lost Leaders   97

10. Bully in a China Shop   109

11. Dishing It Out   143

Epilogue   164

Acknowledgments   167

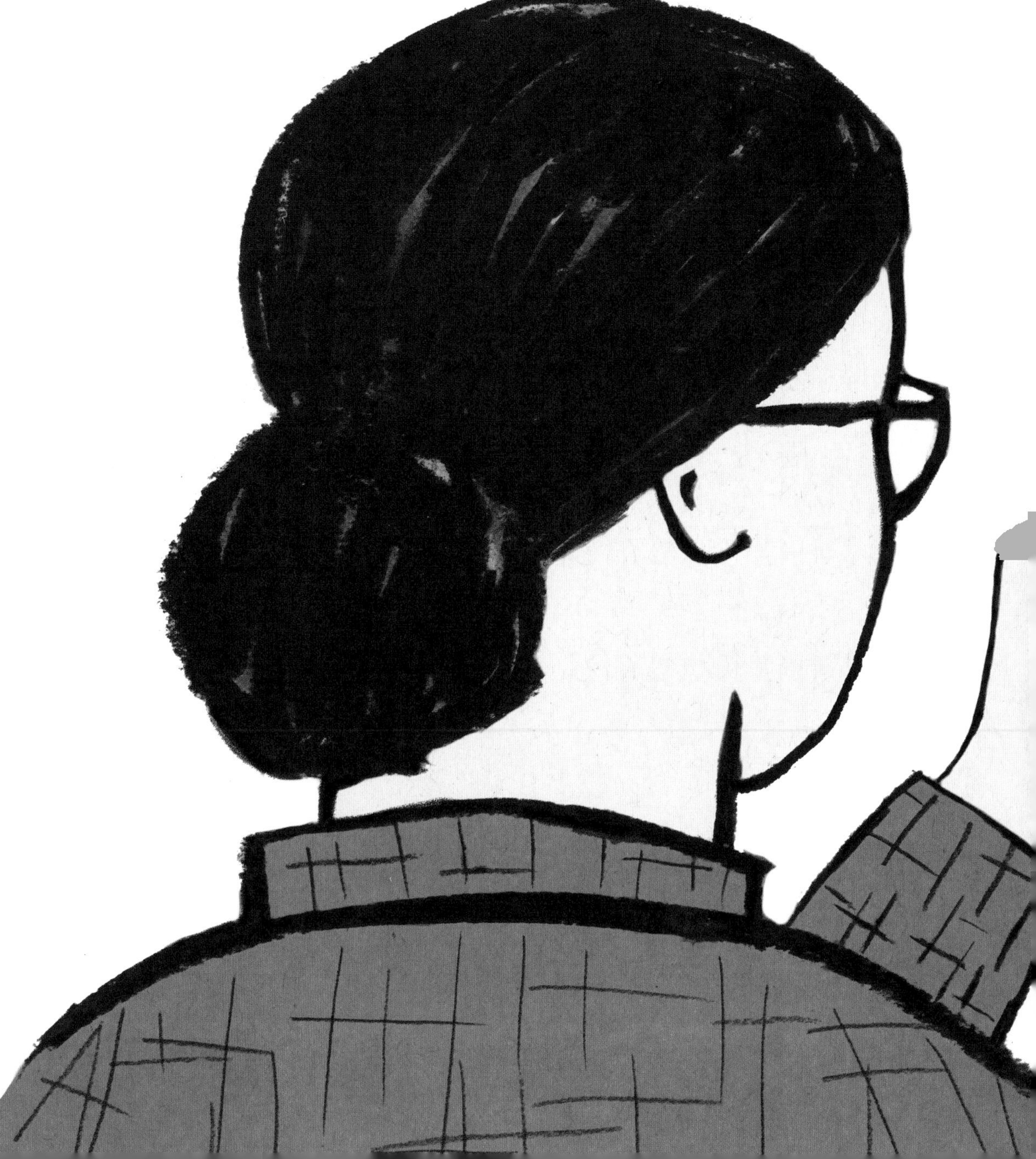

Introduction

A pivotal moment, fifth grade, Staten Island, 1976.

Overhearing my mother's conversation with the saleslady at the jean store while I'm in the changing room.

Mother: She's just impossible to fit.

Saleslady with heavy Staten Island accent: Yuh know, huh problem is she's not petite, she's just really shawt.

I was no particular standout.

Jealous of my two pretty sisters and stuck at 4'11"
when everyone else kept growing, mediocre could
have been my middle name. Instead it's . . . Beth.

But underneath the plaid shirts and clogs, behind the
pounds of makeup I wore on days I was trying to belong,
there inside me was a small spark of certainty that someday,
somehow, I would find a way to fit into this world.

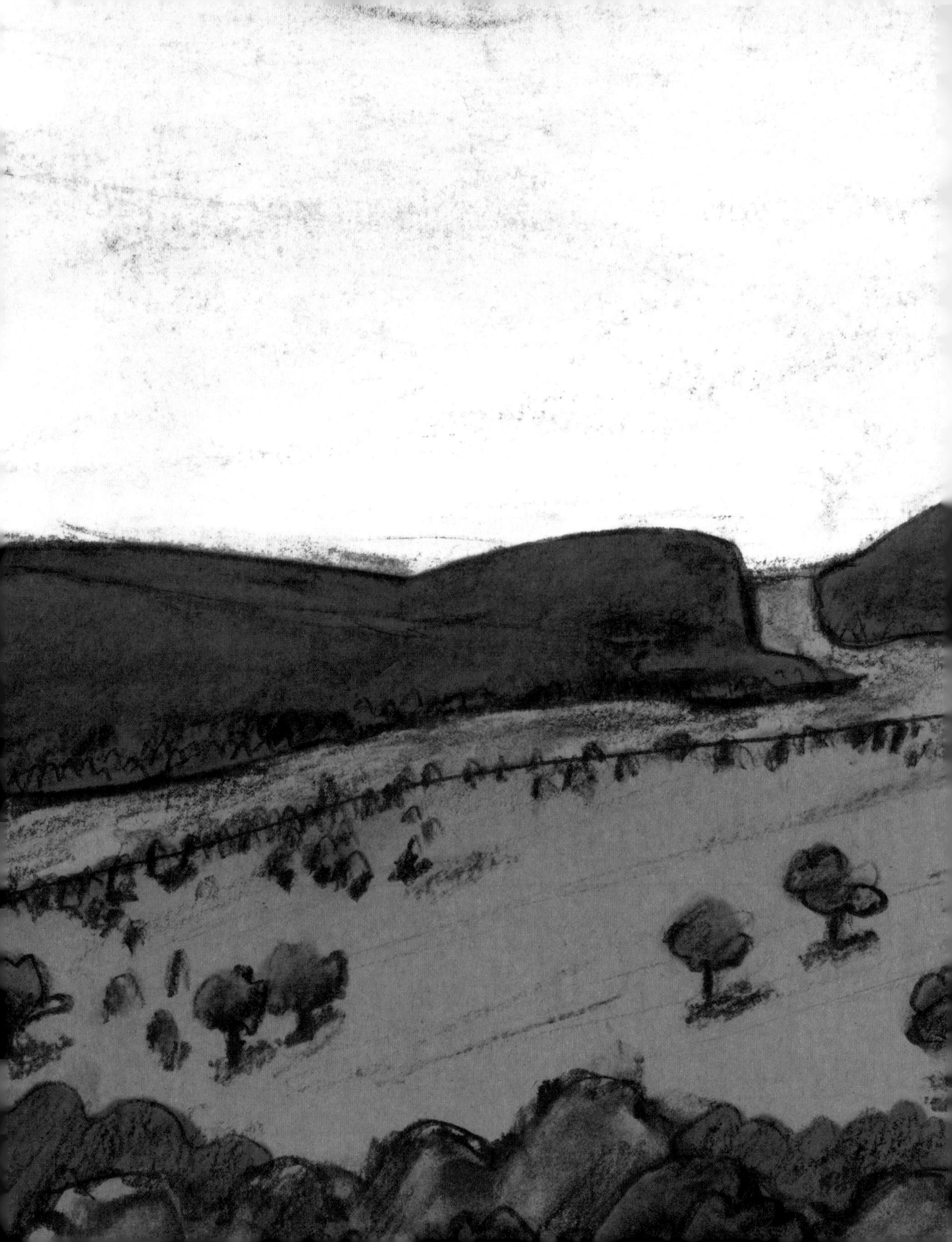

Chapter 1

Road to Fishs Eddy

Soon after college I moved to West 15th Street.
There was a small glassware shop at the end of
the block, so I went in to buy some drinking glasses.

The boy at the register introduced himself as Dave
and said he ran the shop, which belonged to his
cousin. He said the job sort of got him out of trouble.
Whatever that meant. I introduced myself as Julie
and said I had an art degree. Whatever that meant.

Dave told me about his childhood in Miami. He said when his mother invited her friends over for poker night he intruded on their game, often with a dead snake he found in his backyard.

Dave said he was effective at scaring most of his mother's friends, except for the friend who was taking child psychology classes in continuing education and asked if she could do an independent study of Dave's behavior.

Dave annoyed his mother so much that she bought him a one-way ticket to anywhere he wanted. So at seventeen years old Dave came to New York City.

I told Dave how I left Staten Island to study art and that I made the biggest paintings in the class, which apparently didn't make them good paintings, just very big paintings.

That week Dave and I went to see *The Gods Must Be Crazy*, and from then on we were together all the time.

I told my father about Dave but then regretted it, because, while my father didn't have great expectations for me career-wise, he took a profound interest in who I dated.

"An odd man came into the store and bought a useless glass hurricane shade," Dave said a few days later.

All I had to hear was "odd" and "useless."

I haven't sold one of these the entire time I worked here.

Oh no, what did he look like?

Even though my mother said Jewish boys aren't useful in the wilderness, Dave and I decided to go on a camping trip upstate. I told my mother we would be OK because Dave was only half Jewish.

Was he bar mitzvahed?

On the way up to the Adirondacks, we stopped at a Walmart so Dave could buy a survival guide and a hunting rifle. He said we were going to live off the fat of the land. I could see Dave was a real outdoorsman.

WAL☆MART

All Dave did was wound a quail, and I was getting hungry again, so we headed back to the city to eat.

On the way home we talked about how much fun it would be to open up our own shop, and to not have bosses.

We stopped for lunch at a small town called Fishs Eddy and thought that if we did have a store, Fishs Eddy would be a good name even though it was spelled funny.

There wasn't much to see in Fishs Eddy, just a post office and a cemetery.

When we looked at the gravestones in the cemetery we realized that the town must have been named after the Fish family, and someone must have discovered an eddy in a stream somewhere in the town.

I told my mother all about the camping trip and the little town called Fishs Eddy and being with Dave forever.

I knew you'd be back by dinner.

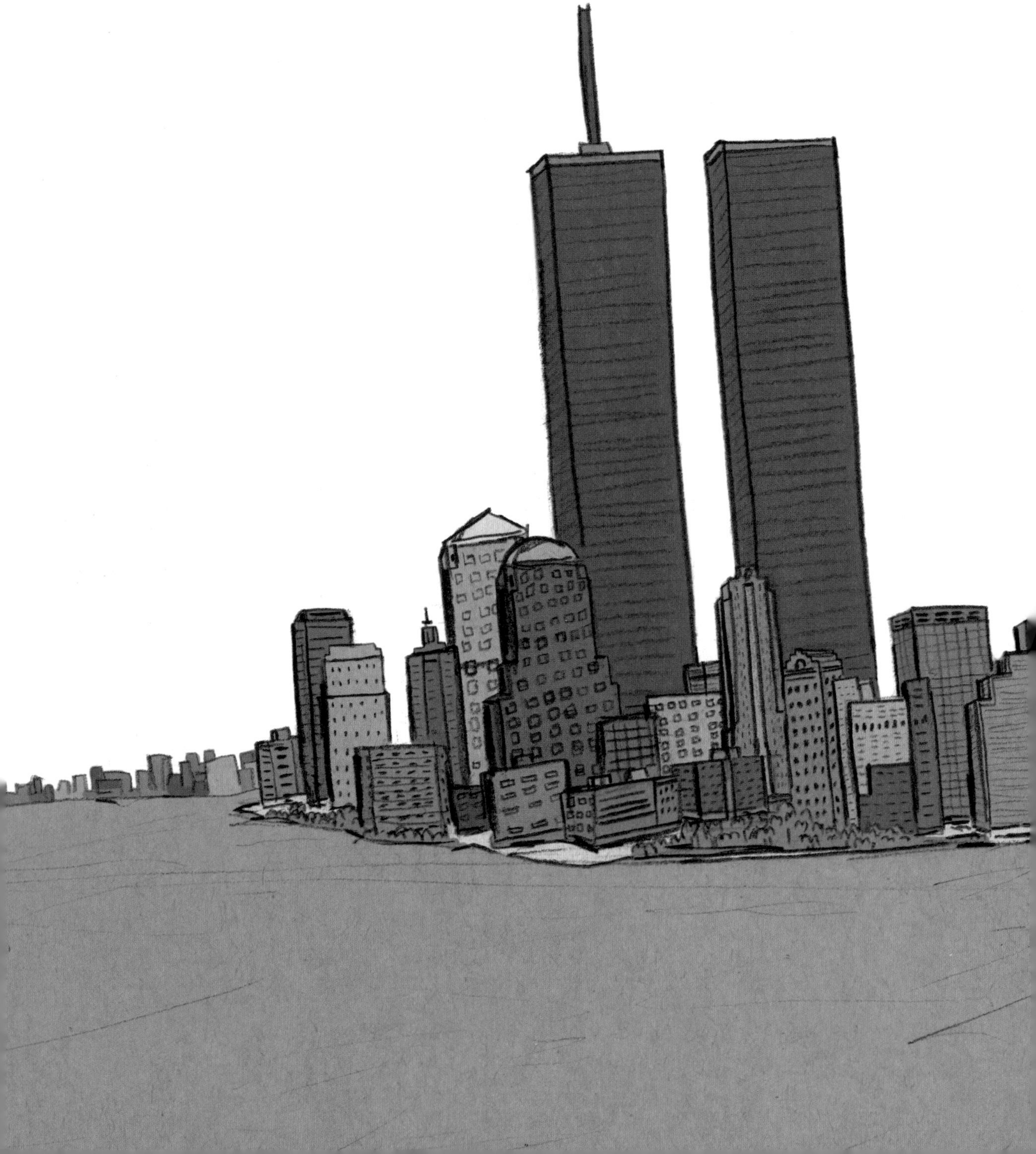

Chapter 2
For Rent

We found a tiny shop near Gramercy Park with a FOR RENT sign in the window. The super of the building said he was sure the landlord would give us a lease. And it would only cost us $100 to talk to the landlord.

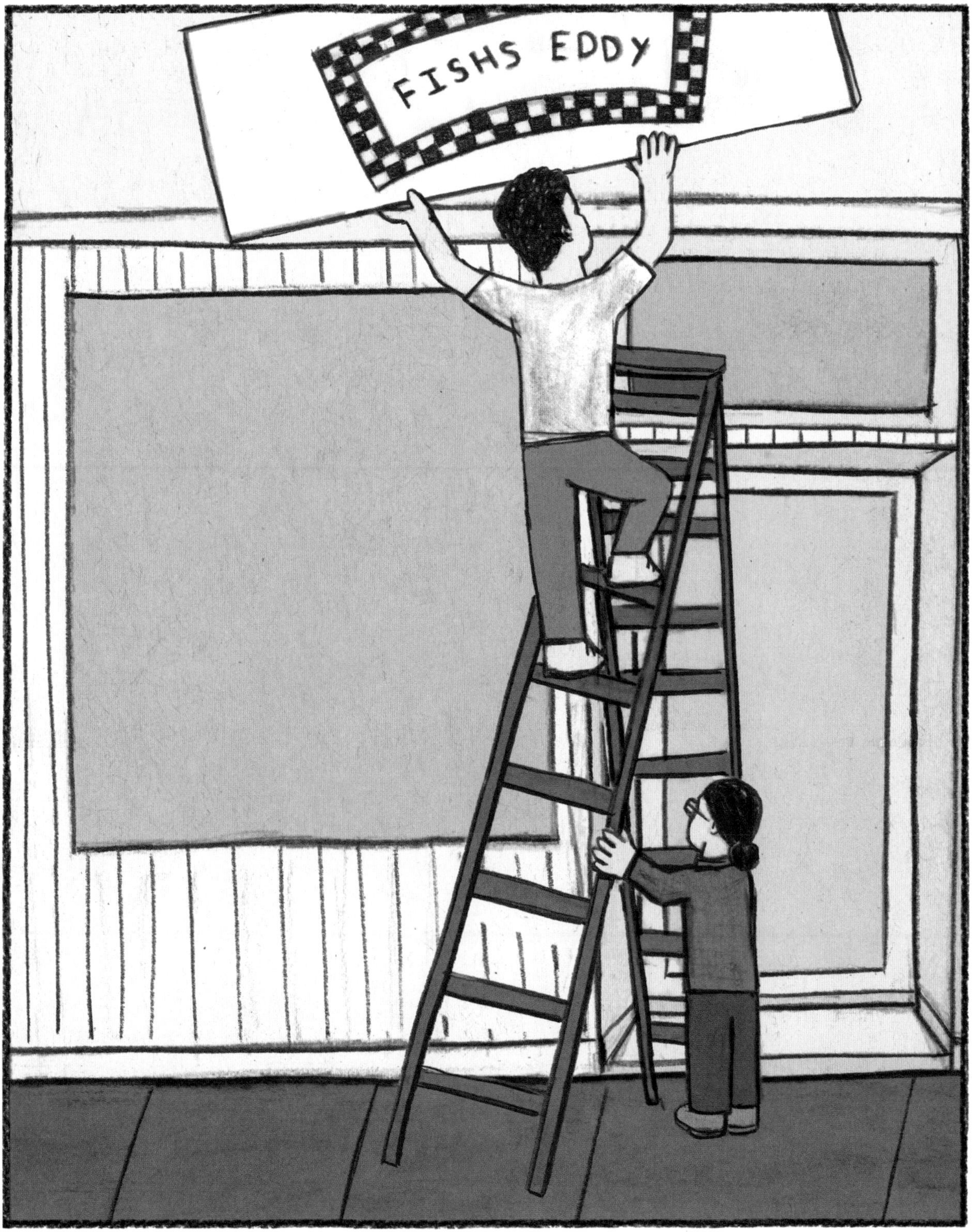
FISHS EDDY

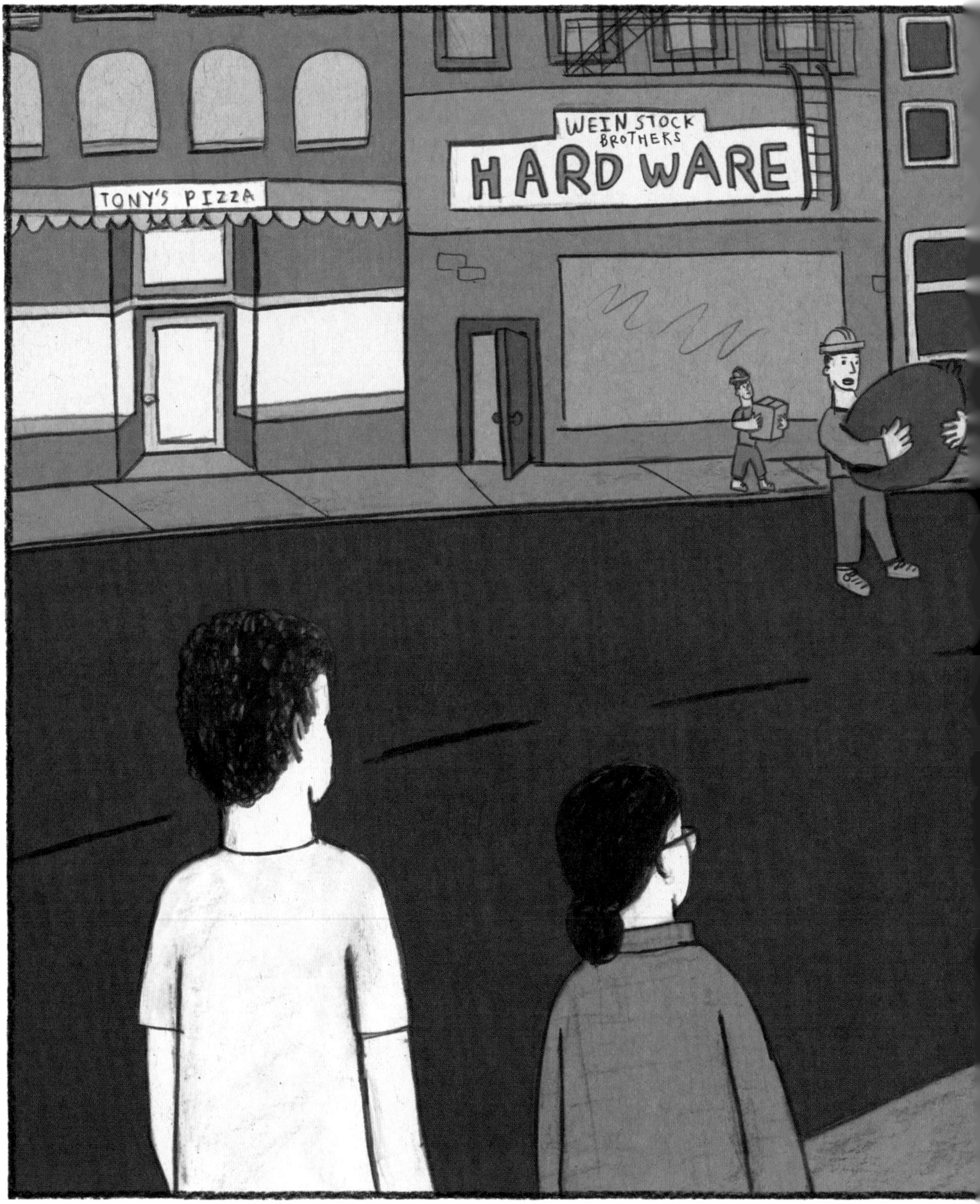
TONY'S PIZZA
WEIN STOCK
BROTHERS
HARD WARE

The following week we walked by a hardware store that was going out of business.

A worker told us the counter was garbage, but for $50 we could have it.

All the old nail kegs and wooden boxes from Weinstock Brothers hardware store made Fishs Eddy look like it had been in business forever.

After we paid the first month's rent we bought a used pickup, and a puppy.

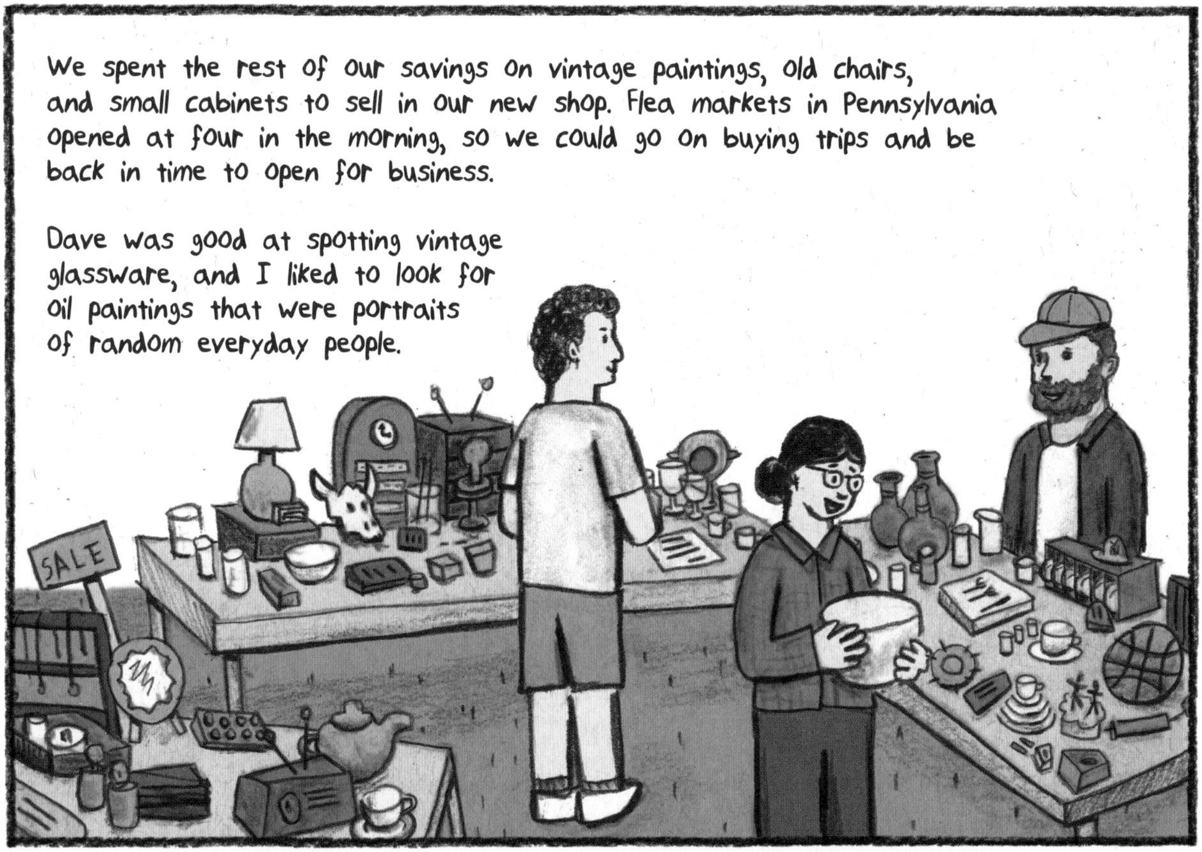
We spent the rest of our savings on vintage paintings, old chairs, and small cabinets to sell in our new shop. Flea markets in Pennsylvania opened at four in the morning, so we could go on buying trips and be back in time to open for business.
Dave was good at spotting vintage glassware, and I liked to look for oil paintings that were portraits of random everyday people.
SALE

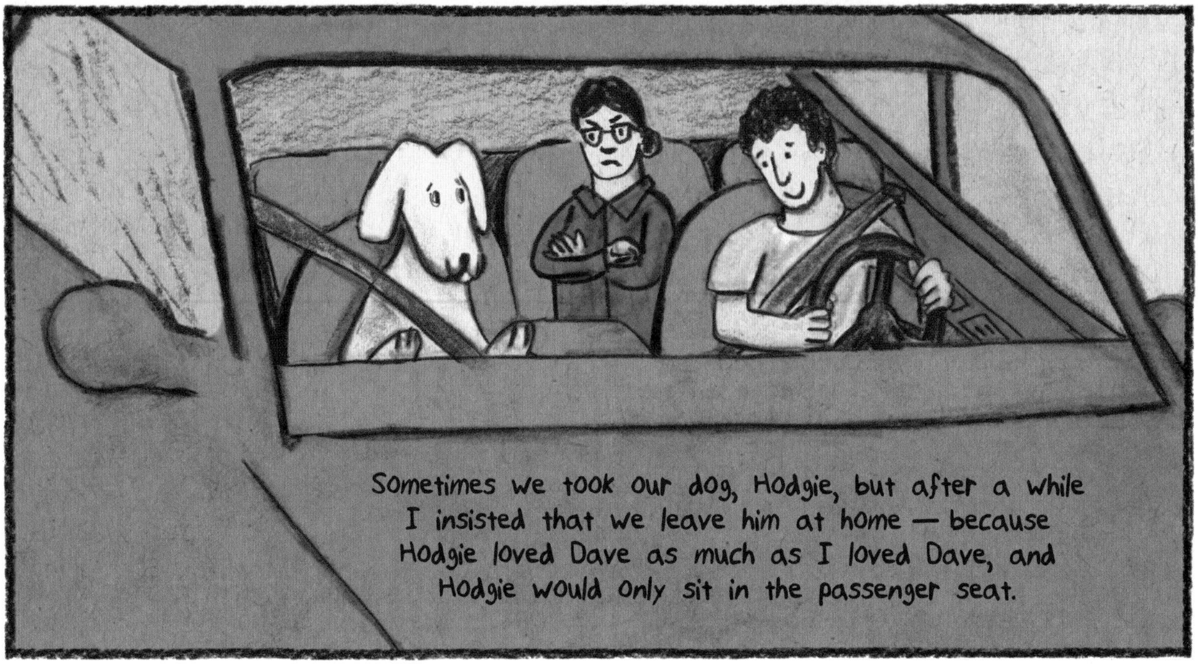
Sometimes we took our dog, Hodgie, but after a while I insisted that we leave him at home — because Hodgie loved Dave as much as I loved Dave, and Hodgie would only sit in the passenger seat.

Dave and I were getting to be experts at flea markets,
but we hadn't yet tried a county auction.

When we left our first auction with a big blue club
chair, which I had proudly won, Dave pointed out that
maybe I shouldn't be so proud, because I had been
sitting in the front row bidding against myself.

After getting a closer look at the club chair
we threw it into a nearby garbage dump
and decided that flea markets were a better
fit for our buying style.

Dave said that I was an auctioneer's dream.
But then Dave said I was his dream too.

Whatever we did and wherever we went, Dave and I were always on the lookout for items we could sell in our shop.

One day Dave spotted an old laboratory cabinet in a Dumpster outside a middle school and hauled it back to the shop. We sold it a few days later.

We even combed through my mother's garage because she saved everything, including gifts she'd received but didn't like.

Aunt JoanBetty came all the way from Virginia to visit my mother, and our store was on her must-see list while she was in New York.

My mother was a gracious host, and Aunt JoanBetty wanted to surprise her with a hostess gift.

So she decided that it would be both wonderful and supportive to buy something for my mother from our store.

Dave and I were happy to get the sale, but my mother was annoyed that we sold Aunt JoanBetty the fruit bowl we had taken from her garage the week before.

Every morning we would take some of our merchandise out in front of the store, as a way to get customers to come inside.

Washington Irving High School was right next door, and at lunchtime students loitered outside until the bell rang. Some of the kids who were smoking cigarettes ignored the bell until they were herded back into the school by security guards.

I had to be careful fixing up our merchandise, because I often got rounded up with the high school kids.

You don't understand! I'm not in school anymore. I have a real store!

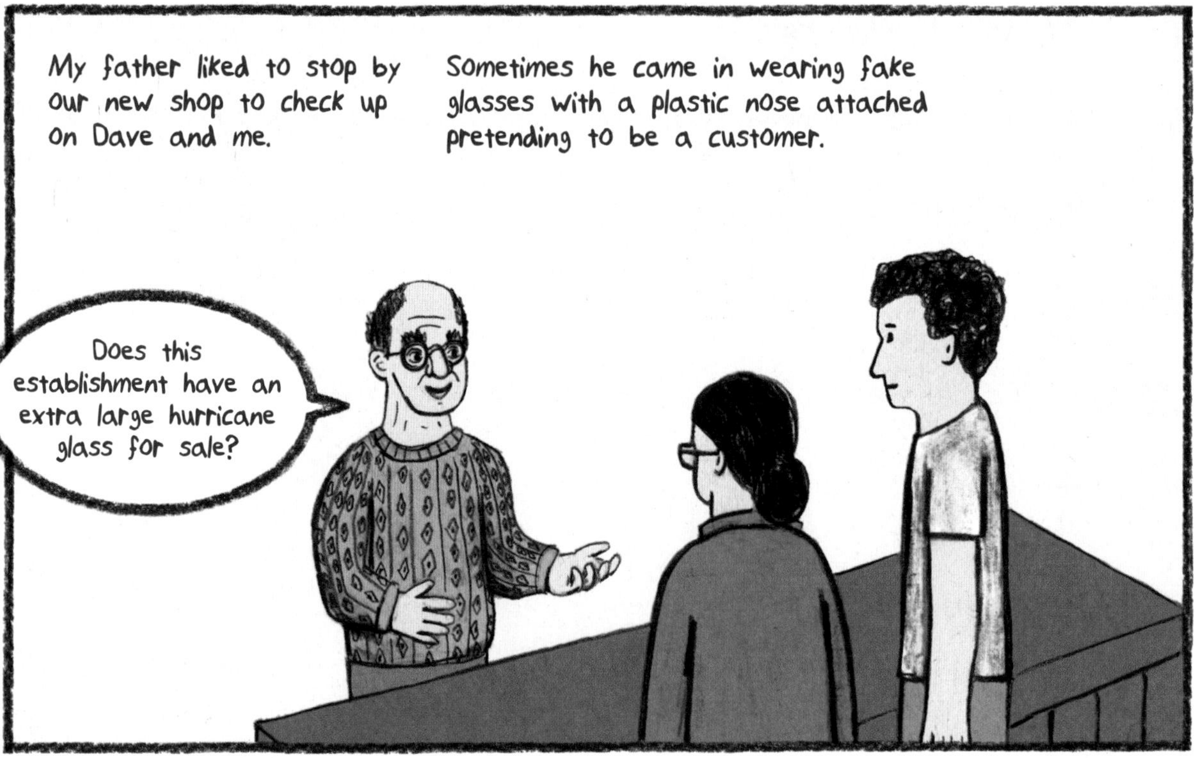
My father liked to stop by our new shop to check up on Dave and me.
Sometimes he came in wearing fake glasses with a plastic nose attached pretending to be a customer.
Does this establishment have an extra large hurricane glass for sale?

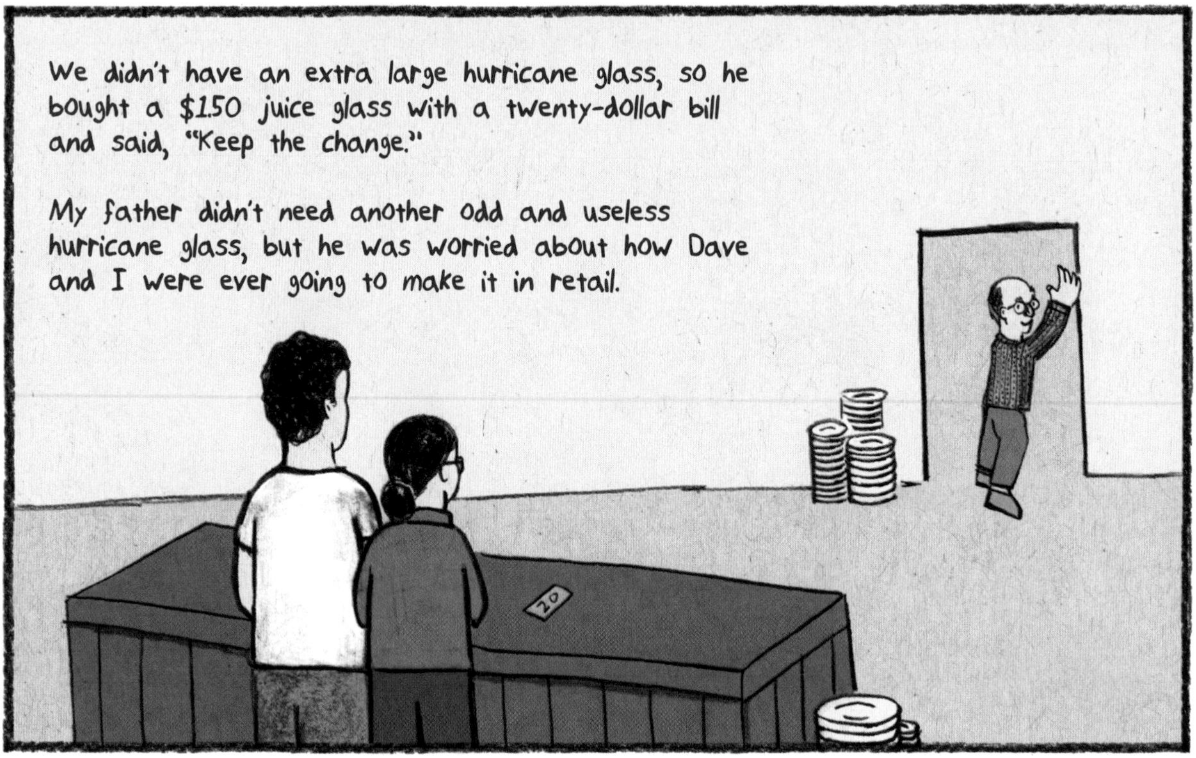
We didn't have an extra large hurricane glass, so he bought a $1.50 juice glass with a twenty-dollar bill and said, "Keep the change."
My father didn't need another odd and useless hurricane glass, but he was worried about how Dave and I were ever going to make it in retail.
20

Dave and I were very young to be shopkeepers, and we were very happy too.

We even made a GONE FISHING sign that had nothing to do with fishing, or Fishs Eddy, and more to do with . . .

Chapter 3

Doing Dishes

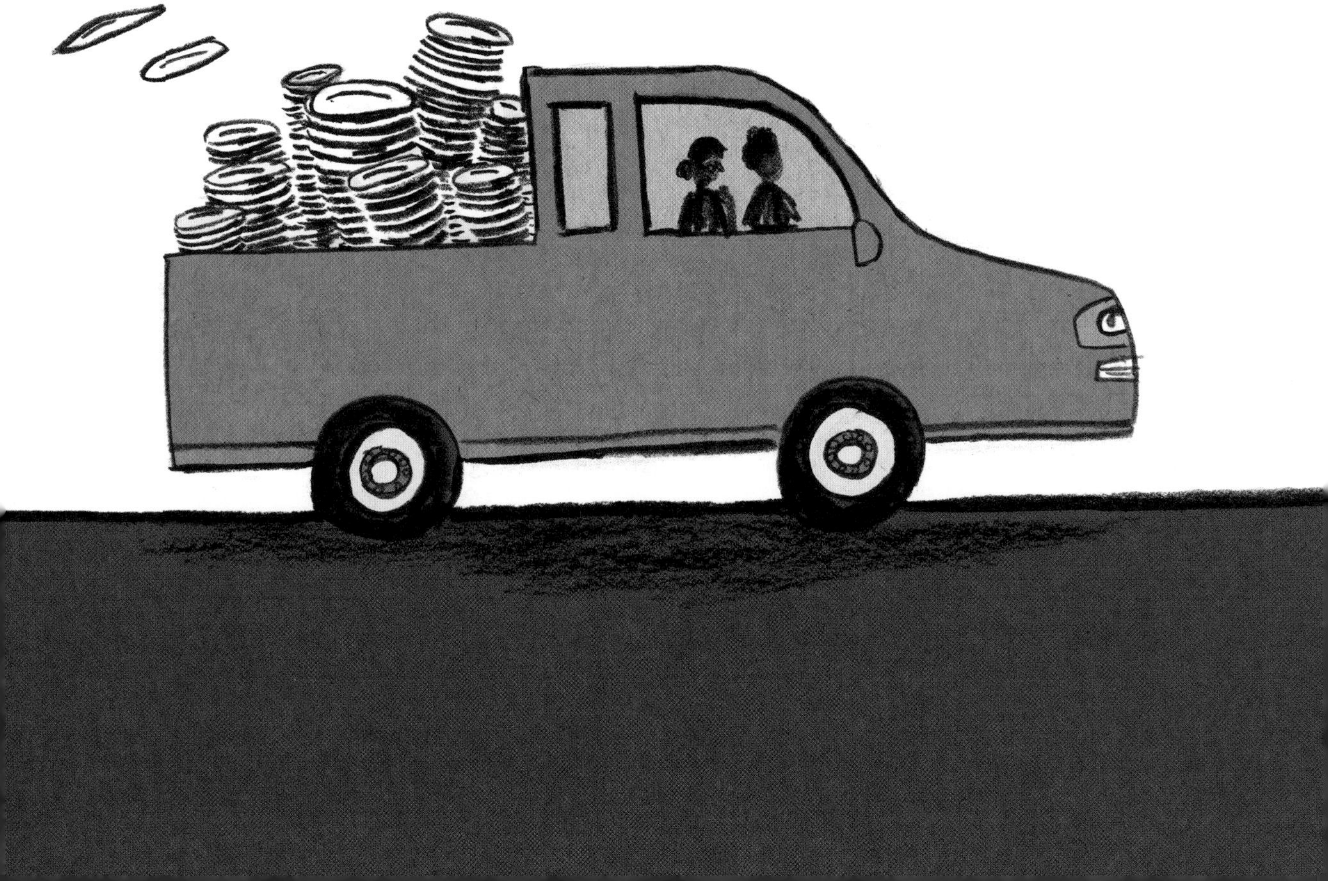

Some of the Jewish immigrants who came to America in the 1930s peddled dishes and glasses to the boom of restaurants and hotels popping up all over the country. Eventually their pushcarts became a cluster of businesses that formed a restaurant supply district along the Bowery in New York City.

Most of the buildings were narrow five-story walk-ups with basements and sub-basements. It was a part of the city with so much history.

The little glassware shop where I met Dave sold some restaurant dishes, which was unusual, because retail stores didn't sell dishes from restaurants.

Dave and I were inspired by that, so we went down to the Bowery to look for more restaurant dishes to sell in our own shop.

The salesman in the first restaurant supply business we walked into told us we could take a look in his basement.

He said his basement was filled with random dirty dishes that were outdated and obsolete, and why would we want those? But he did have a really great deal for us on a ten-burner gas range with two twenty-six-and-a-half standard ovens, and he would throw in free delivery to our restaurant.

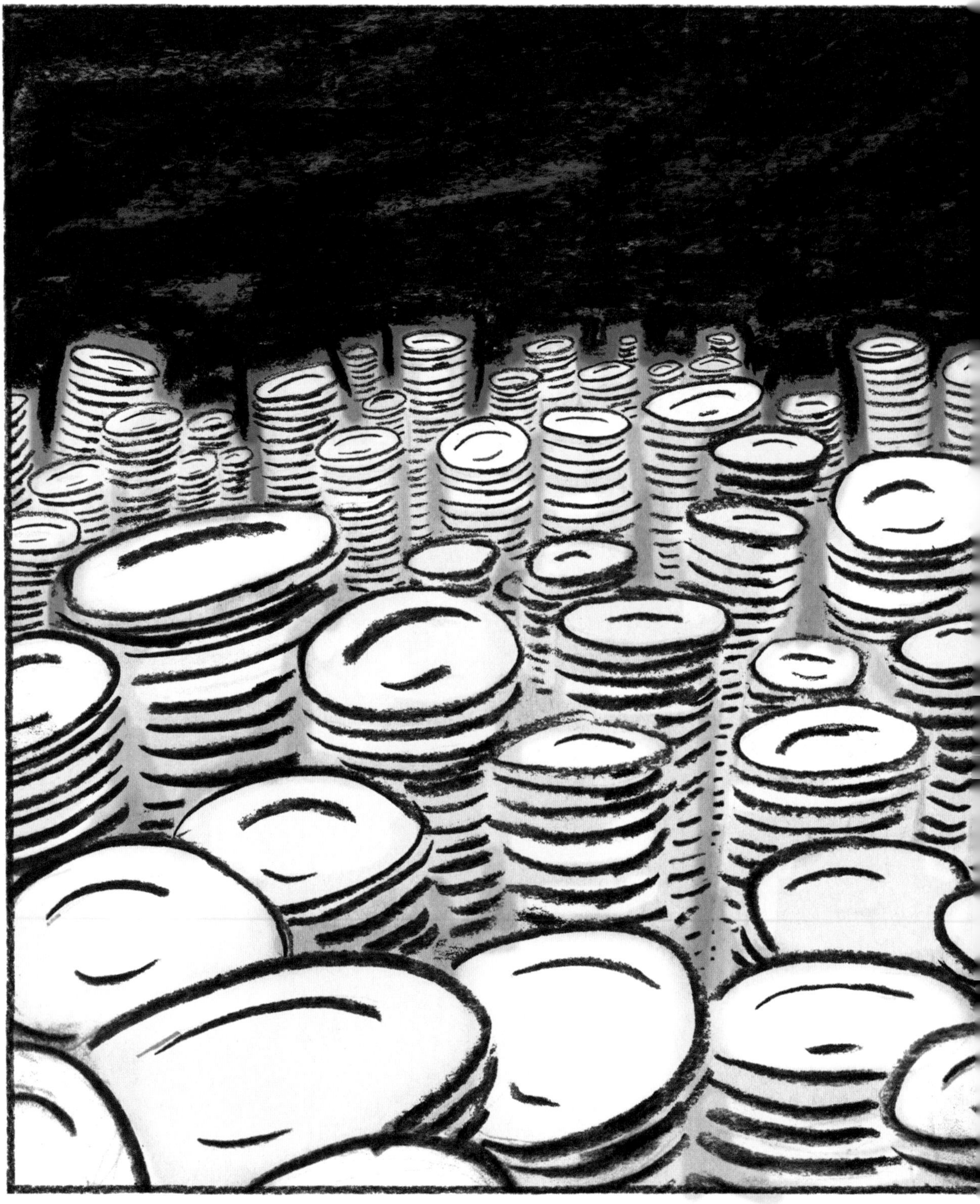

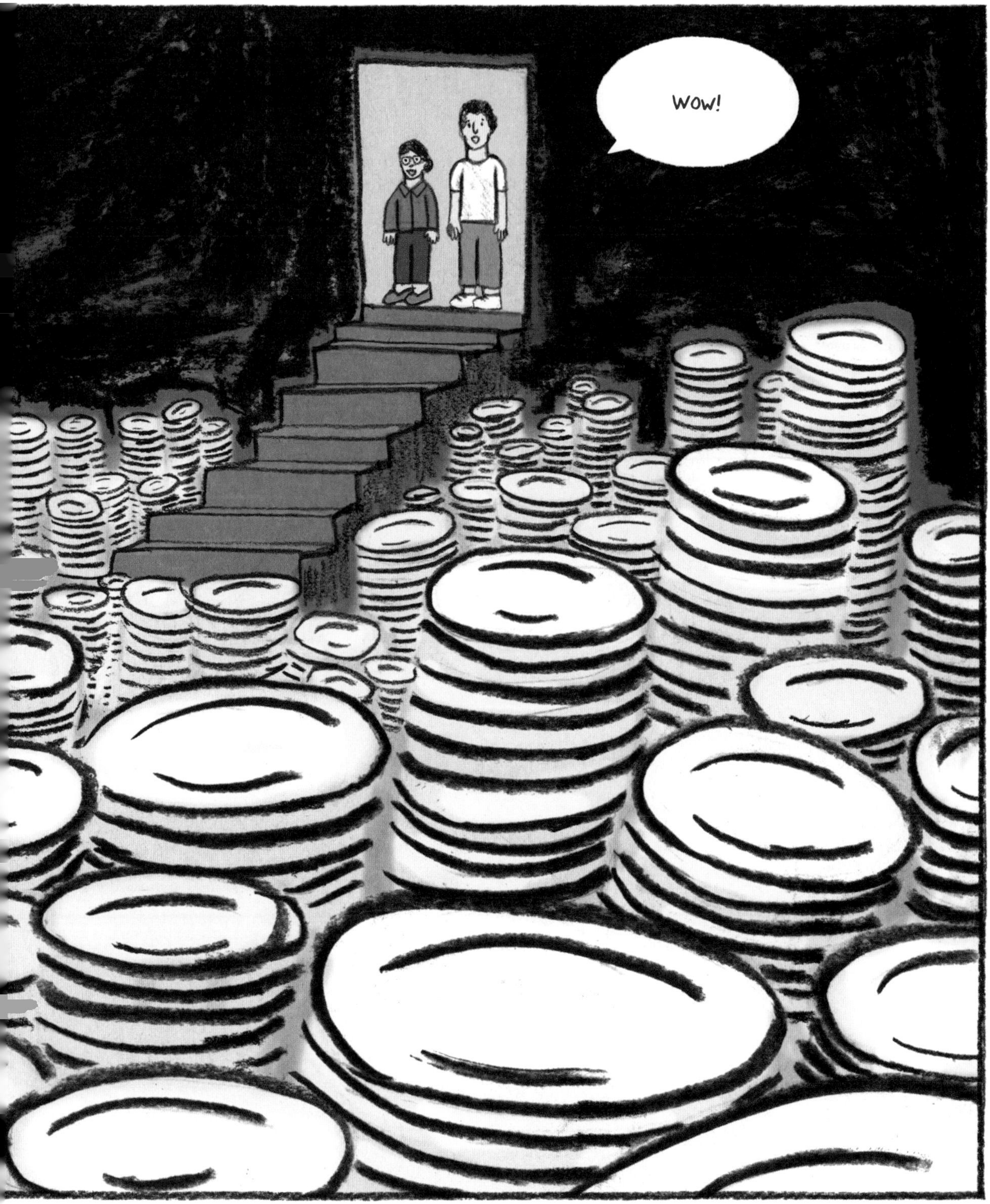
WOW!

There in the basement were thousands of stacks and endless bushels of soot-covered dishes dating back to the 1900s! The sub-basement had even more!

It didn't take long to discover that almost every basement along the Bowery was filled with unwanted "wares." We went every day, from basement to basement, digging for old creamers, butter pats, mugs, bouillon cups, and plates.

The basements were dank and scary, but we were amazed to be down there with our flashlights rubbing off dirt, discovering dishes from old hotels, diners, schools, and railroads.

Many of the dishes were so caked with gunk we couldn't identify where they were from until we took them back to the store to clean and price them.

There were soup bowls and celery dishes from Howard Johnson's and Bickford's diner and Bernstein's Fish Grotto. We found mugs from country clubs and masonic lodges and steakhouses.

The Astor Hotel platters looked like they belonged in a museum. Dave and I were unearthing a slice of American history!

Dave never forgot my enthusiasm while bidding for the blue club chair at the county auction. He always reminded me to be discreet and act like I didn't care about the dishes or else we would get charged a lot.

But we never got charged a lot, because we were doing the hard labor of clearing out the unwanted stock of these restaurant suppliers in the Bowery.

KING'S
RESTAURANT SUPPLY

Oven Fryer, Food Safety,
Service Mans, Bartending
Dishwasher, Equipment

Bowery

Canal

Some of the suppliers were curious about Dave and me. We became known as "that young couple" who showed so much interest in the old dishware acquired ages ago by their fathers and grandfathers.

Nobody else seemed to care about all those dirty dishes.

Repeat customers and new customers started coming in every day to see our latest finds.

There were so many dishes for customers to discover. The dishes were selling fast, and if a dish didn't sell fast, we simply hid it under a table.

I was eager to share the history of the dishes with customers, but I became more careful after I made the mistake of telling a lady the cup she was buying was very old, from the fifties.

Oh really? I too am from the fifties!

New York magazine wrote an article praising Fishs Eddy as the best new shop around.

The day the article came out we made our rent in just a few hours. After that I started calling a lot of newspapers and magazines to tell them about the vintage restaurant ware at Fishs Eddy.

Dish Must be the Place

FISHS EDDY

Cups and saucers blah blah blah vintage china-ware

Best Store around BLah Young couple Blah Blah Bla FISHS EDDY

plates and mugs blah blah BLAH

With all the press we were getting, the name Fishs Eddy was gaining recognition. So when we read in the *Post* that a brand-new restaurant called Fish and Eddie was opening uptown, we contacted the owner and asked if he would please reconsider the name, because we were already getting calls asking if Fishs Eddy had a children's menu or if Fishs Eddy served halibut and if so were we aware that halibut was on the endangered species list?

Despite all the calls to Fishs Eddy for reservations at Fish and Eddie, the owner refused to consider our plea. Eventually Fish and Eddie closed and a new restaurant called Vince and Eddie opened, in the same location.

Yes, Smith, table for four. We'll see you at eight.

Dave and I both loved how we were surrounded
by an unsung part of everyday life in America.

Nobody really thought about the cup they drank coffee
from every morning at a local coffee shop, or the platter their dinner
was served on at their favorite steakhouse, yet somebody somewhere
in the clay belt of Ohio had stood on an assembly line, adhering
handles to mugs or applying decals to dinner plates.

Dave loved that we could go early each morning twelve blocks south to the Bowery, haul hundreds of plates back to our store, and be our own bosses.

I loved how much fun it was displaying and merchandising the dishes, and how our little business was becoming an indelible part of New York City.

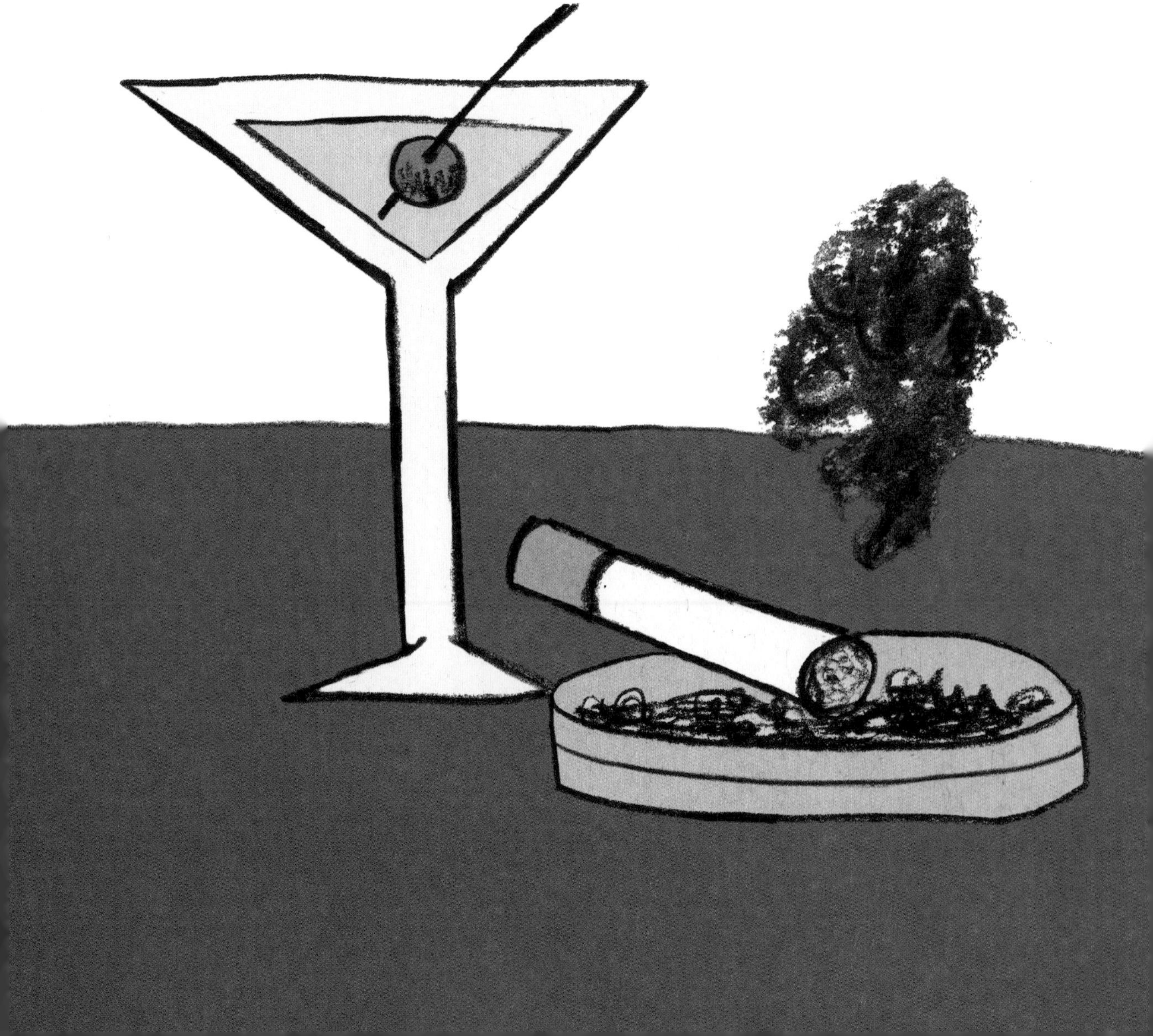

Chapter 4

Customer Service
in the Early Years

After a few years in the Gramercy Park store, we moved to a better location on Hudson Street in the West Village, a much busier part of the city. The new space was no more than five hundred square feet, so there wasn't need, or room, for salespeople.

But shortly after we signed the lease, Dave and I listened in horror as our mothers announced that they would be running the shop.

Both of our mothers lived in New York City at the time and were excited about their new jobs.

Dave's mother was a tall Irish woman
with a sharp tongue, a throaty voice, a martini
in one hand, and a cigarette in the other.

She had a preference for gay men and resented
straight men — including her own son.

You know I lost all
respect for you when
you married him.

My mother was a short Jewish woman who was raised in the Deep South, but she had spent her adult life on Staten Island, so she had access to two different accents.

My mother used her Southern voice when she went on gambling cruises with her best friend, Phylma, but she used her Staten Island voice when she ordered extra-lean corned beef with full sour pickles.

From day one our mothers' employment came with stipulations.

"I'm shutting down early on Wednesdays. That's when I do lunch and theater with the girls," my mother would clarify.

"And by the way I want two weeks' cash in advance in case you don't make enough to cover my salary," Dave's mother would explain.

Boy George is gay now? Oy, what next!

But when it came to customer service, our mothers had completely different approaches. My mother had a don't-make-eye-contact-with-the-customer method.

She kept her face buried in a magazine while customers were privy to her informative thoughts on important issues of the day.

Shoplifters in particular liked to frequent the store during my mother's shift.

But it was hard to reason with her.

People

Mom you have to look up from your magazine once in a while. They didn't even steal dishes this time — they stole the microwave from the back of the store!

Well, apparently they would rather have a microwave than your dishes!

Dave's mother had her own special brand of customer service, often resulting in a more hostile environment.

On the rare occasion when Dave and I dared to call the store during her shift, she would bark into the receiver, "Just wait!" Then we would overhear her finishing up with a customer.

I didn't ask you to come in here, did I!?

When our bank statements arrived each month Dave discovered that one man in particular kept writing bad checks. Dave's mother was positive she could identify the culprit the next time he wrote a bad check, so she and Dave devised a plan to catch him.

Ma, as soon as the bad-check-guy comes in, call me on the phone and tell me that you need more mugs.

That will be our secret code so I know to come and catch him in the act.

Dave's mother was excited to solve the crime, so for the next few days she paid attention to the customers.

When the man finally showed up, she distracted him by being pleasant.

You know you can buy that cheaper at Pottery Barn.

Dave's mother called immediately to relay the secret code, but Dave had forgotten their arrangement.

PSST! Get me mugs NOW!

Mom, since when do you care about inventory?

The problem was solved when the man stopped shopping at the store because he couldn't get good customer service.

A lot of celebrities shopped at Fishs Eddy. Dave's mother was especially thrilled to wait on Diane Keaton.

"So, Ma, what did you say to her?" Dave asked nervously. "I told her that she looks much younger on the big screen. Now stop bothering me here."

Dave and I decided that we needed to be firmer with our mothers.

Ma, please, no personal calls.

Please keep it down. Marie is telling me something important about her cats.

In spite of both mothers, business grew. We hired a perky young woman named Beverly as a third salesperson.

Hello, and welcome to Fishs Eddy.

Beverly was happy and cheerful toward customers.

Oh, come on. You've got to be kidding me.

But we knew Beverly was never going to be their role model. We needed a plan.

We replaced our tackle box with a real cash register.

How the hell do you work this thing?!

We scheduled deliveries during their shifts.

Now I have to stand here and hold the doors open?

Dave and I decided to call a staff meeting. Me, Dave, Beverly, and our mothers.

Uh, we were just noticing that Beverly seems to have mastered good customer service.

Not that you two aren't completely charming.

Eventually work overwhelmed both mothers and they moved on.

Mine to the gated communities of Boca Raton.

BOCA MALL

And Dave's to the gay communities of Pompano Beach.

In their brief but distinguished careers at Fishs Eddy, they proved one thing.

Our dishes would sell themselves.

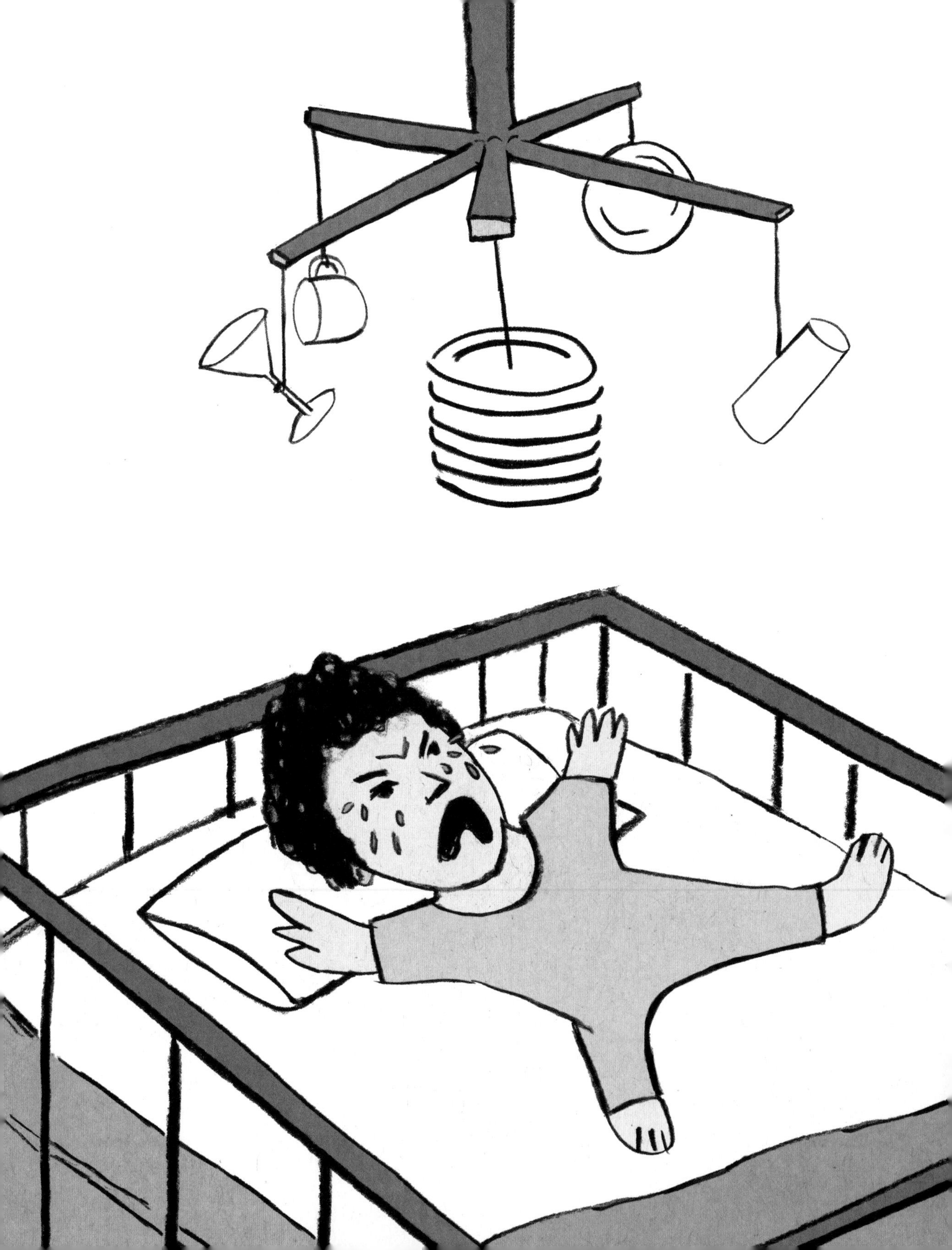

Chapter 5

Family Business

Dave's younger cousin Noah knew a lot about running a store because his father owned the little shop at the end of 15th Street where Dave got his start, and where I met Dave.

Noah worked with us during summer breaks in college, which was helpful now that our mothers had retired from retail. Dave and Noah liked to clown around and wrestle a lot, but then Noah got bigger and started winning.

Each morning we dragged an old green park bench out to the sidewalk in front of the store. The bench became a popular hangout for neighbors in the West Village.

One customer who was often at the green bench came into the store and bought an entire truckload of random dishes.

When Dave returned from delivering them he told me the man was an artist who said his name was Julian Schnabel and he wanted to break all the plates and use them in his art. Dave and I laughed, because it's hard to break dishes made for restaurants.

Two Chinese brothers owned the tiny newsstand right next door to our store. The brothers told us that they wanted to give themselves popular American names, so they chose Cecil and Milton. The large one was Cecil and the skinny one was Milton.

Cecil and Milton's grandfather stood guard all day and night, shooing away people trying to steal their newspapers. We wished our mothers could have witnessed the way Cecil and Milton's grandfather handled customer service and loss prevention.

For Chinese New Year we gave Cecil and Milton some dishes as a gift, but our sentiment must have gotten lost in translation because the next day our gift was displayed in the window of their newsstand, for sale.

While their English wasn't great, we had an unspoken camaraderie with Cecil and Milton . . . because we were all shopkeepers on Hudson Street in the West Village of New York City in the 1980s.

FISHS EDDY

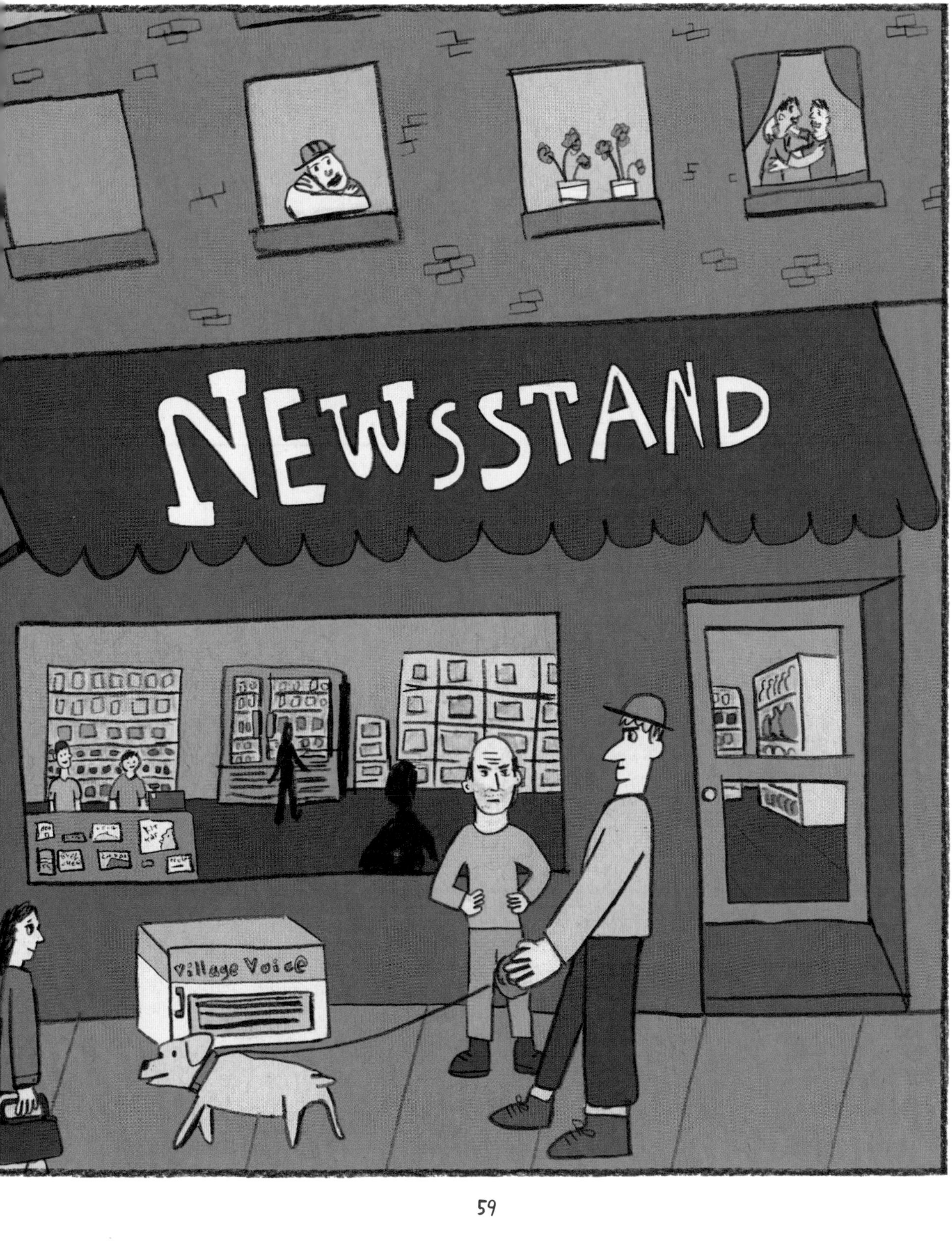
NEWSSTAND
Village Voice

Dave and I weren't particularly skilled at planning, which included family planning, so when we had a baby who didn't stop crying for six months we wondered if we should have thought things out a little more.

We were constantly shouting just to hear each other. Ben's colic was so traumatic that Dave and I pinky swore we would never procreate again.

He's crying because he has a diaper rash!

If we ever get a divorce, you get custody!

Hope, who worked at the store, offered to help us with Ben. After a few times babysitting, Hope and I started flipping a coin to see who got to work the cash register and who had to watch Ben.

Hope stuck it out for a few years with Ben, but then she started getting religious.

I'd start believing too if I had that job.

We didn't think Hope's newfound beliefs were an issue, until one day when we called home.

Ben wasn't crying at that moment so Hope put him on the phone.

Hi, Mommy I'm making a house of worship!

Dave and I decided, now that Ben was a little older, that Hope was probably a better fit for the register.

The pediatrician said one reason Ben cried a lot was because he was allergic to Hodgie, and that made him itchy and uncomfortable. So we said goodbye to Hodgie, and kept Ben.

The day Hodgie was picked up by his new family, Dave had colic too.

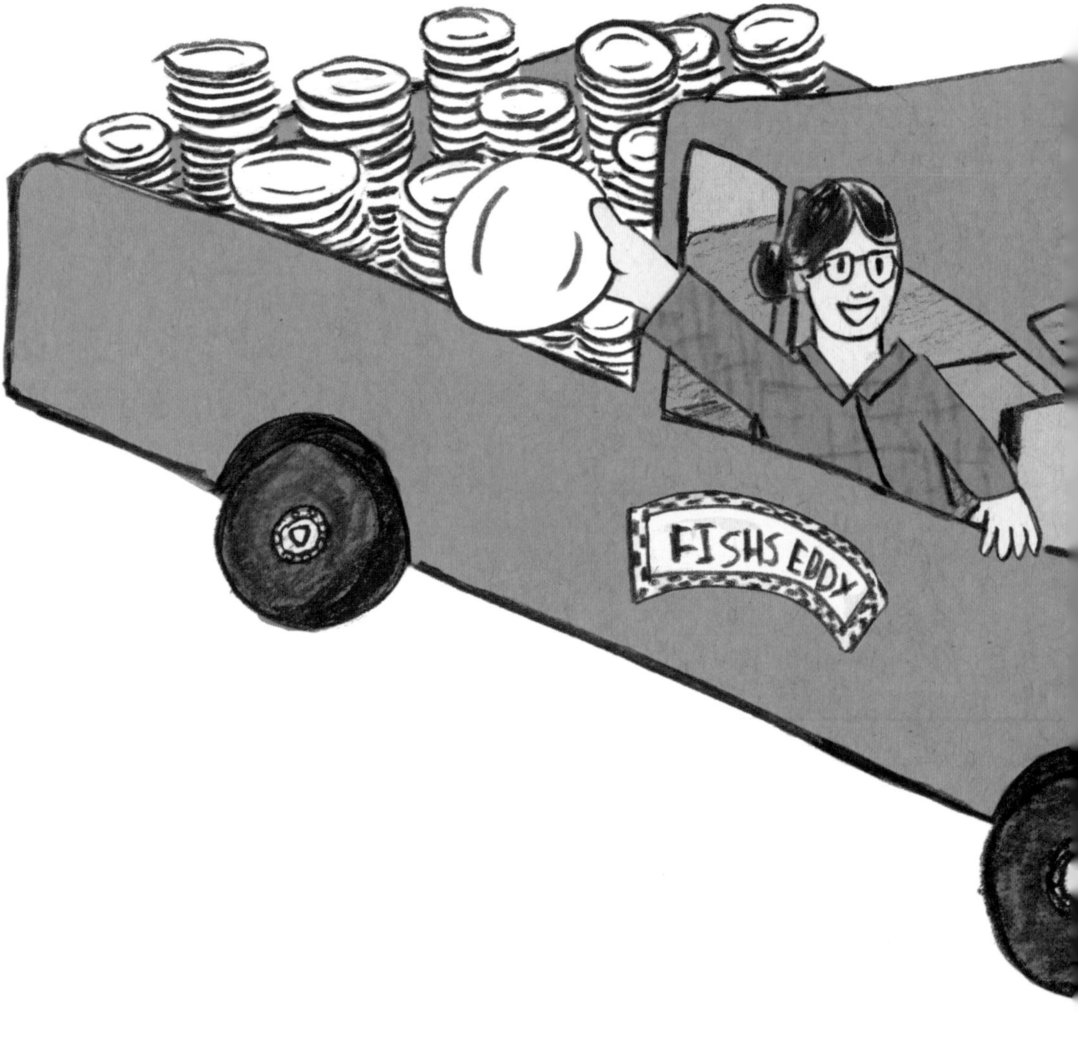
FISHS EDDY

Chapter 6

Road Scholars

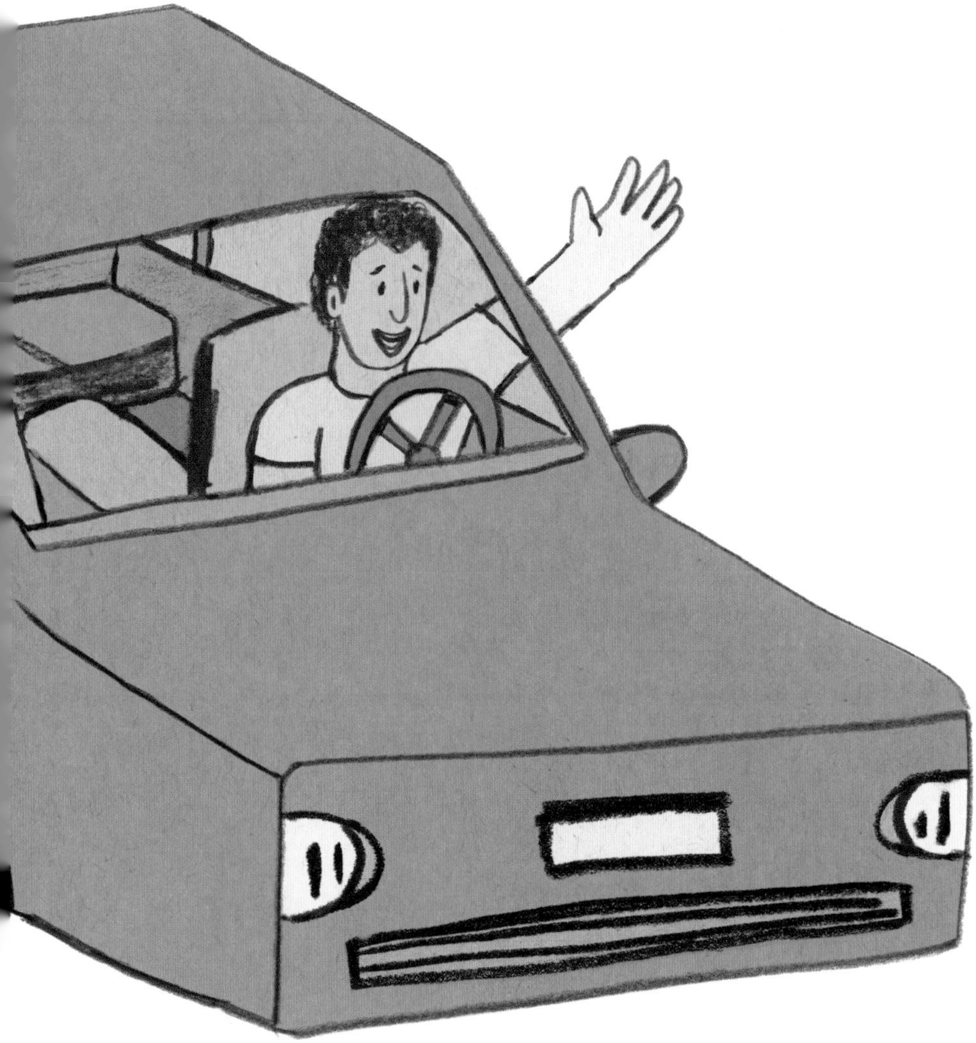

Noah finished college, and his Fishs Eddy summer job
turned into a full-time job, which turned into
a partnership with Dave and me.

Dave and I accidentally broke our pinky swear to never procreate again, and we had a little girl named Susie. Susie instinctively knew it was in her best interest to smile a lot and to not have colic.

Dave and Noah spent a lot of time out on the road buying dishes, and I spent a lot of time in the store merchandising, which meant I could be home at night for Ben and Susie.

Our roles were evolving, our merchandising was evolving, and without paying too much attention to what a "brand" meant . . . that too was evolving. We started expanding our product line and our assortment, even designing our own dishes.

One morning while I was sitting at a diner with Dave, I drew a quick sketch on a napkin of a silhouette of the New York City skyline.

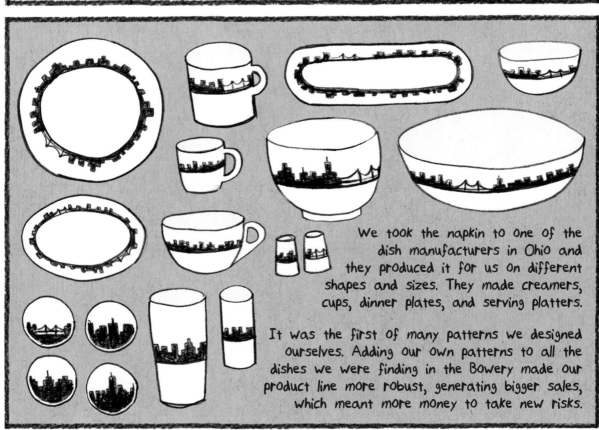

We took the napkin to one of the dish manufacturers in Ohio and they produced it for us on different shapes and sizes. They made creamers, cups, dinner plates, and serving platters.

It was the first of many patterns we designed ourselves. Adding our own patterns to all the dishes we were finding in the Bowery made our product line more robust, generating bigger sales, which meant more money to take new risks.

I sent a note to a well-known fashion designer named Cynthia Rowley, asking if she would consider doing dishes with us. The worst she could say was no, but I was hoping she would say yes, because Cynthia Rowley had an edgy New York style.

Cynthia was intrigued by the idea so she invited me to her West Village studio to talk about a dinnerware line called Fashion Plates. It was the first of many collaborations with outside artists. The collaboration with Cynthia Rowley made me feel like a real fashion plate!

Our reputation for selling vintage restaurant ware was growing so much that we started getting calls from establishments looking to get rid of their old dishware.

The food and beverage manager at the Helmsley Palace called about the hotel's basement full of outdated dishes still in their boxes. He needed the dishes out as soon as possible.

It was perfect timing. We got thousands of teapots and rectangular serving platters with the fancy gold Helmsley Palace Hotel logo just as Leona Helmsley was in the news every day for federal income tax evasion.

A former housekeeper testified that Leona said, "Only the little people pay taxes."

We did a window with the Helmsley Palace dishes and a sign that read NOW THE LITTLE PEOPLE CAN EAT.

The New York Times liked our window, so we became news too.

We were always getting calls to take unwanted stock, and we were always on call to take it.

What we ended up hauling back to our store was usually a surprise. It was fun to be in the basement of the 21 Club because it was once a speakeasy. On the way home from clearing out dishes at the Harvard Club, Dave and I joked, "Yeah, who's smart now?"

Around the middle of the 1990s many domestic ceramic manufacturers were closing their doors for good. It was becoming too expensive to make dishes in America, and few manufacturers were left standing.

To Dave and me, it didn't seem possible. These were factories that had been around since the turn of the century, family businesses that went back generations. They had made the bowls to feed immigrants coming through Ellis Island and the teapots that had graced railroad dining cars when railroads had dining-car service.

These were the factories that had made all those dishes we excavated from all those basements in the Bowery. And these were the factories that had taught Dave and me to never take "Made in America" for granted.

Jobs were lost, pensions were lost, and millions of dishes were to be thrown into Dumpsters. The only way we could justify benefiting from such misfortune was to continue our commitment to making Fishs Eddy into a business that offered jobs and benefits, and that hopefully could even one day give back.

Dave and I pledged to each other we would soon be that business.

When a factory closed, Dave and Noah did everything they could to salvage what was going to be destroyed.

They rescued a giant map of the United States with hundreds of tiny orange pushpins representing thousands of business accounts across the country.

They salvaged original decal books, cup molds, sample plates from factory archives, carts used to push heavy dishes around the plant, and old cabinets.

When I opened the cabinets to use them as store fixtures, I found family photos, little shaving mirrors, work schedules, and calendars attached to the inside of the doors. Because those weren't just cabinets . . . they were the lockers used by American factory workers.

With so many plates, creamers, mustard pots, and bouillon cups passing through, Dave and I were building a personal collection of vintage dishware. Dave was passionate about the dishes made for the US military and I loved our collection of creamers made for hotels.

One morning on the way to school Susie asked, "How much money can I get for all those dishes when you and Daddy are dead?"

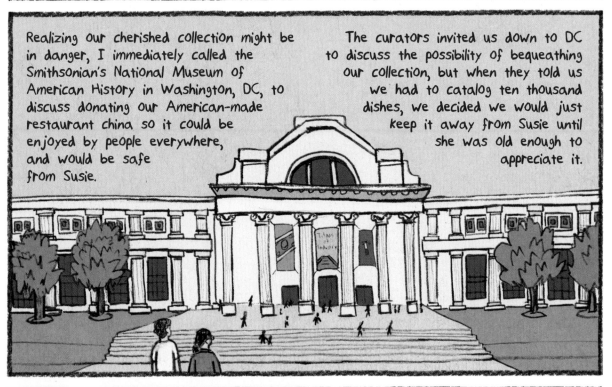

Realizing our cherished collection might be in danger, I immediately called the Smithsonian's National Museum of American History in Washington, DC, to discuss donating our American-made restaurant china so it could be enjoyed by people everywhere, and would be safe from Susie.

The curators invited us down to DC to discuss the possibility of bequeathing our collection, but when they told us we had to catalog ten thousand dishes, we decided we would just keep it away from Susie until she was old enough to appreciate it.

On the way out of the museum we were excited to see that the Smithsonian had its own Astor Hotel platter displayed in a showcase. Dave and I had unearthed many Astor Hotel platters years ago in the Bowery.

Chapter 7

In the Black

The sight of FOR RENT signs in empty storefront windows triggered strange and euphoric feelings in me. Dave was able to walk right by a FOR RENT sign, but I didn't find it so easy. FOR RENT signs meant opportunity to display more dishes and turn Fishs Eddy into a bigger business.

The FOR RENT sign in a store near Union Square was different though. Dave and I both knew to call and inquire. It was a large corner store with interior columns, a mezzanine for offices, and a real co-op board that needed to approve us. It was not at all like the tiny shop we were used to.

You don't sell fish do you?

Plans for the future?

Do you have loud children?

Can we get Fishs Eddy discounts?

Despite the phone calls from our mothers telling us how the Union Square area would never amount to anything, we signed the lease.

Dave's sister made invitations for the opening party in our big new Broadway store and everyone came — family, friends, neighbors from the West Village store, and editors from magazines. Our mothers were proud and gracious hosts, going from guest to guest explaining how they taught us everything we know about retail.

It wasn't the kind of opening I had dreamed of a long time ago when I was in art school. It was even better!

It was okay that we were amassing more dishes than we could sell. These dishes were true artifacts!

Dave's mother always had a deep passion for real estate. When Dave was a little kid, she dragged him to open houses to see three-bedrooms with sunken living rooms and aboveground pools whenever they were announced in the local newspaper.

OPEN HOUSE

Dave's mother was never buying real estate, but she was always looking.

So with his "inherited appreciation" for real estate, Dave found an old Studebaker showroom on Staten Island and convinced the Small Business Administration to give us a loan to buy it with hardly anything down — which was good because we had hardly anything to put down.

The warehouse was ages away from the dressing room at the jean store my mother took me to in fifth grade, but only a ferry ride away from Manhattan, which was good, because I hated driving.

I felt bad that Dave was always the designated driver, but Dave said he loved that position, and that it had nothing at all to do with the buying trip when I insisted on driving but then accelerated into the car in front of us minutes after taking the wheel.

Dave and Noah renovated the entire warehouse and even built an outlet store on the first floor so we could sell some of those dishes we had way too many of.

We put a big sign on the front of the building: NOW INTERVIEWING EXPERIENCED SALES ASSOCIATES. INQUIRE WITHIN.

A lady named Helga finally came in asking for the job. The warehouse was in a rough neighborhood, so whoever said yes was the winner.

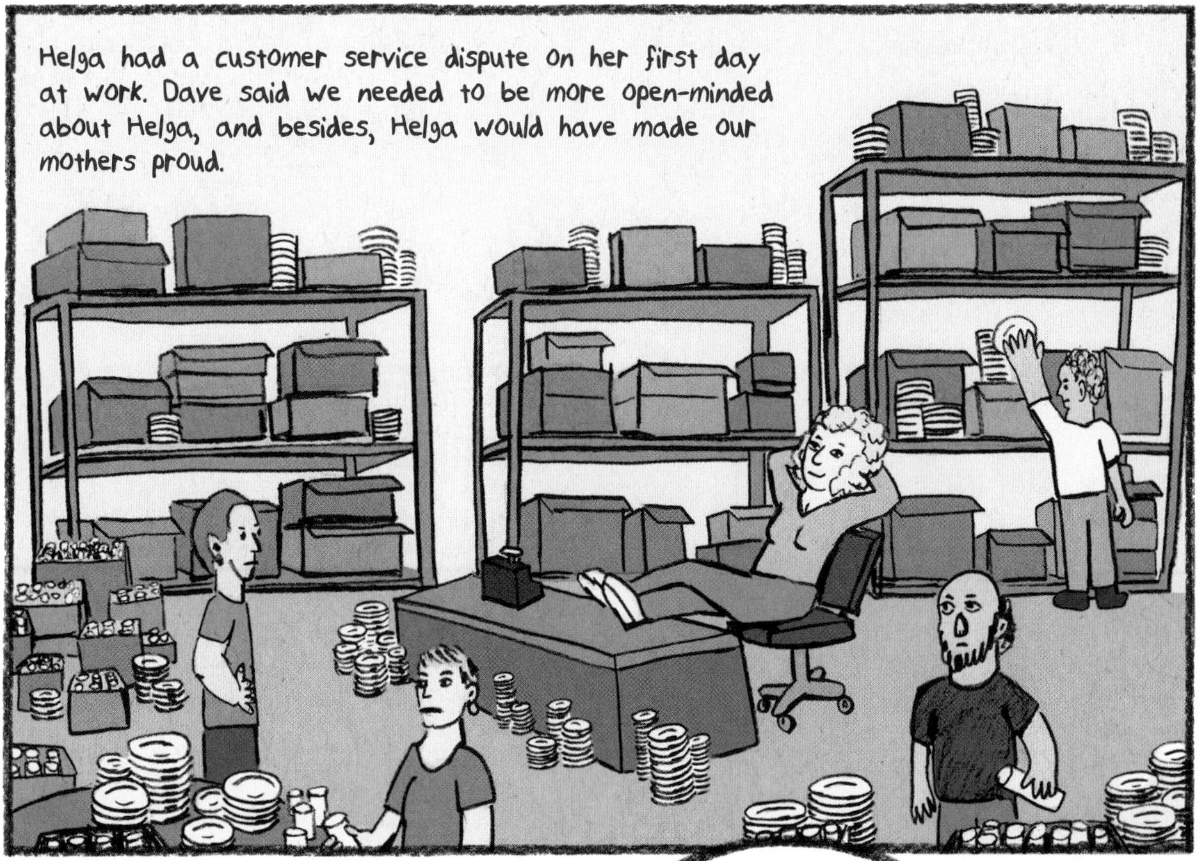
Helga had a customer service dispute on her first day at work. Dave said we needed to be more open-minded about Helga, and besides, Helga would have made our mothers proud.

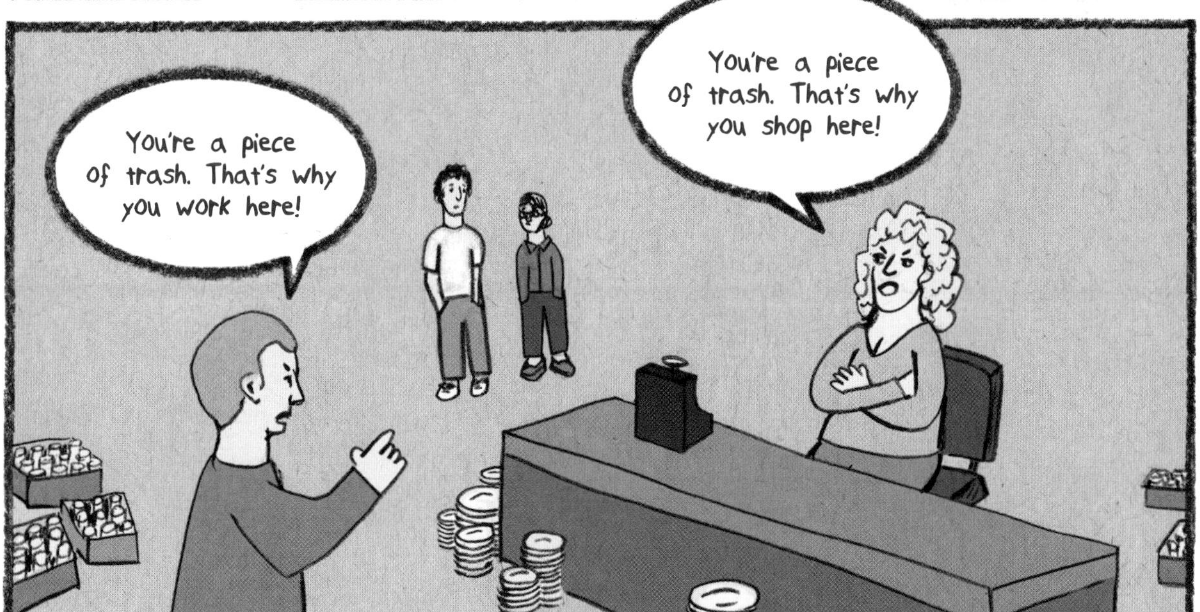
You're a piece of trash. That's why you work here!
You're a piece of trash. That's why you shop here!

Dave and I thought that since business was good it might be time for us to give back. Restaurants in the city came together to form charities that helped feed the homeless. Our idea was to get retail stores working together to help the New York City public schools.

Ben went to a good public school, but public schools never had enough money for library books or after-school programs or soap for the bathrooms.

Since we knew that most retailers were always short on extra cash, we hoped to persuade them that their generosity would be good for their businesses. They didn't have to give much, and their stores would be part of a big campaign with lots of publicity and marketing going to a good cause. Dave came up with the perfect name — Shop 4 Class.

I was sure everyone was going to sign up, but it was a difficult sell.

Taking risks, trying new things, and approaching new people had been working for us. So writing a letter to Caroline Kennedy, who was head of the Fund for Public Schools, was another chance worth taking. I told my sister Ilene all about the letter to Caroline Kennedy, because I told my sister everything and she told me everything.

A few days later I answered a phone call and heard, "Hello, this is Caroline Kennedy," and I said, "Shut up!" assuming it was Ilene pretending to be Caroline. But then I only heard silence.

Shut up!

Caroline was enthusiastic about Shop 4 Class and invited me to her office at the Tweed Courthouse next to City Hall to discuss the idea.

Caroline said I should tell the retailers who were hesitant that they were all invited to her office and that she would personally ask them to sign up for Shop 4 Class. Everyone wanted to meet Caroline Kennedy, so it was a full house.

Shop 4 Class became a real event, with billboards and commercials on TV.

Caroline even went on a morning show to talk about how the proceeds would go to public school libraries.

I was very proud when I took the M20 bus near our apartment downtown and saw Shop 4 Class advertised at the bus stop.

Susie started kindergarten at P.S. 89, a few blocks from the World Trade Center. On her first day of kindergarten I started my new routine, walking her to school and catching the 9 train underneath the World Trade Center.

Just as the subway doors were closing a man jumped down the full flight of stairs and dashed into the train. He said that a small plane had accidentally hit one of the towers.

When I got out of the train at 18th Street, there was a sea of people facing south in disbelief. Because it was no small plane, and it was no accident.

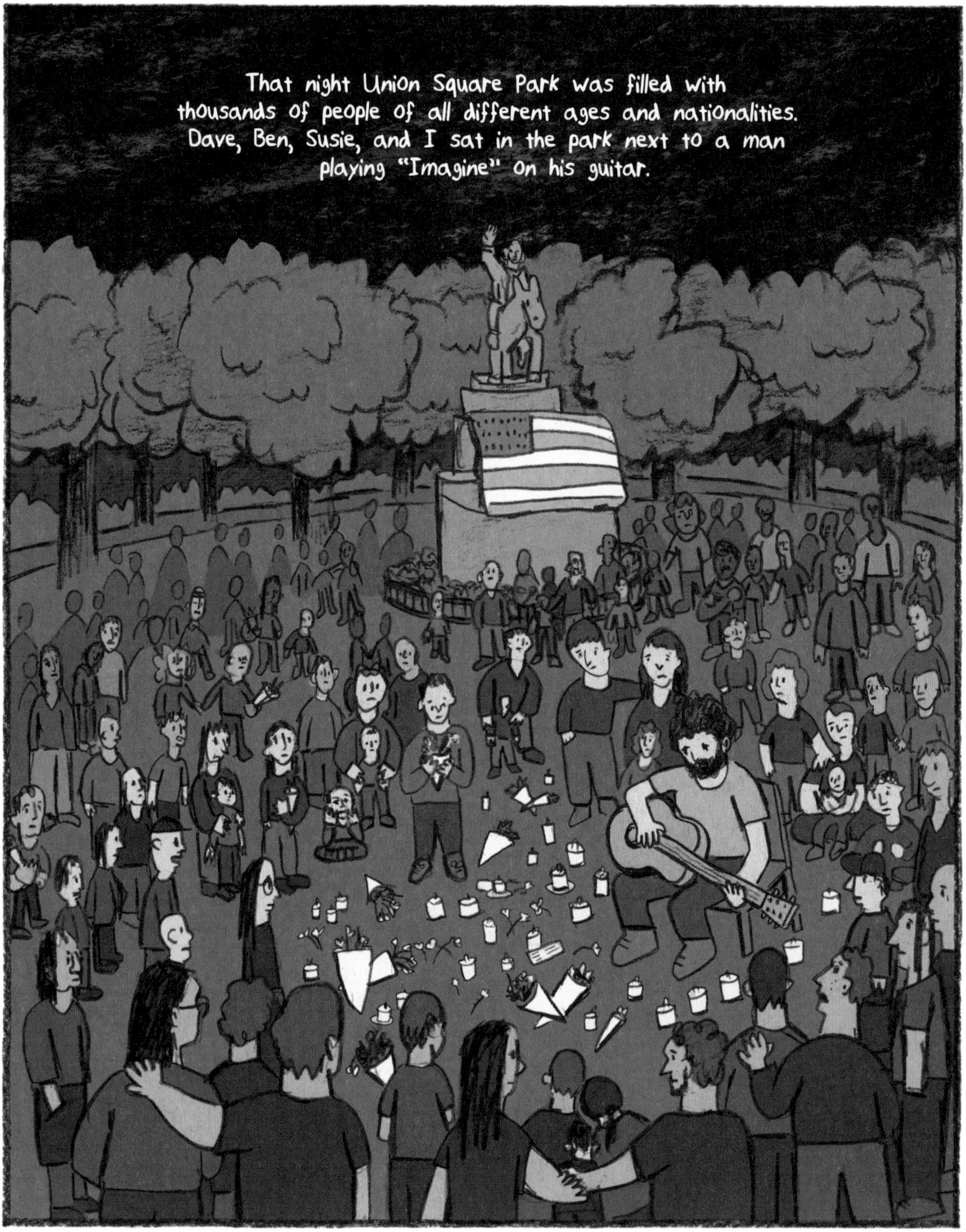
That night Union Square Park was filled with thousands of people of all different ages and nationalities. Dave, Ben, Susie, and I sat in the park next to a man playing "Imagine" on his guitar.

On the morning of September 12th we walked together as a family to the store. From the end of the block Ben and Susie pointed out that there were flowers and lit votive candles in a makeshift shrine left outside Fishs Eddy's corner window.

We didn't understand why there would be candles and flowers at the store until we got closer and saw that the little memorial was left outside the window because our New York City Skyline dishes were displayed inside.

After such a tragedy my mother called and said she wanted to fly from Boca to be with me. "I just want to be with my baby!" she cried into the phone.

When my mother arrived, I said, "What kinds of things do you want to do together?"

I'm sorry, honey, I'm busy every night — Broadway tickets are half price to encourage people like me to go to the theater and get back to normal after the tragedies of 9/11.

Other small businesses had to close because of the terrorist attacks, but sales of our New York City Skyline dishes kept Fishs Eddy going . . . and we all appreciated the irony in that.

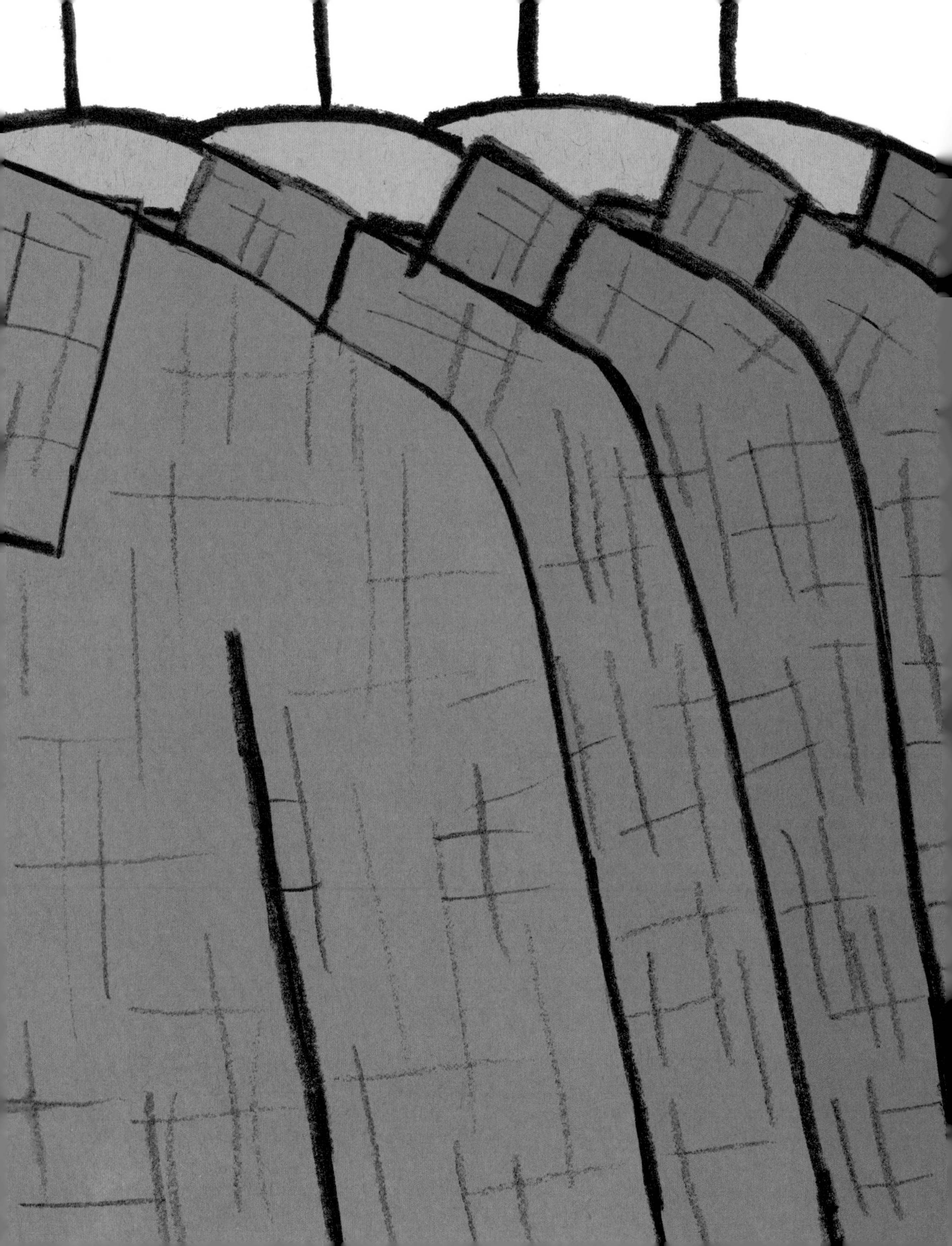

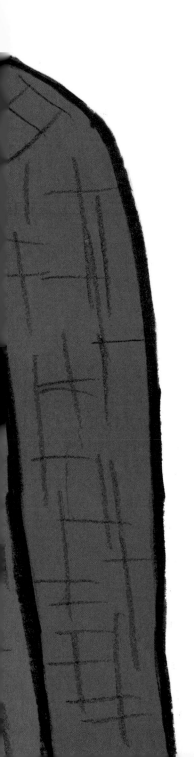

Chapter 8

Half-Baked

Dave and I tried to keep schedules like other families, but it was a challenge to separate Fishs Eddy life from family life. Over the years my mother came often to visit us from Boca. She was wary of our accommodations, so she traveled with her own sheets, towels, blankets, and throw pillows for an added home touch.

My mother was especially annoyed when she saw that we had no dishes in our apartment.

I told her if she wanted to see dishes she should come to our warehouse, but she said she couldn't because she and Phylma had tickets to see Matthew Broderick on Broadway.

I explained to my mother how we either ate out or ordered in because we were usually too busy to make dinner.

Have you noticed that they run when they hear a doorbell because they think it's food?

My mother didn't even understand how we could let Ben go all by himself to the corner to get dessert at Nuts 4 Nuts. We told her it was safe, and besides, Ben was getting a worldly education, because Manolo from the Ivory Coast managed the Nuts 4 Nuts stand, and Manolo was Ben's best friend.

I offered to cook lemon chicken for my mother, or what Dave, Ben, and Susie called fifty-fifty lemon chicken, because there was a 50 percent chance that it was cooked all the way through. Ben and Susie liked the chicken and knew to eat the parts that were fully cooked.

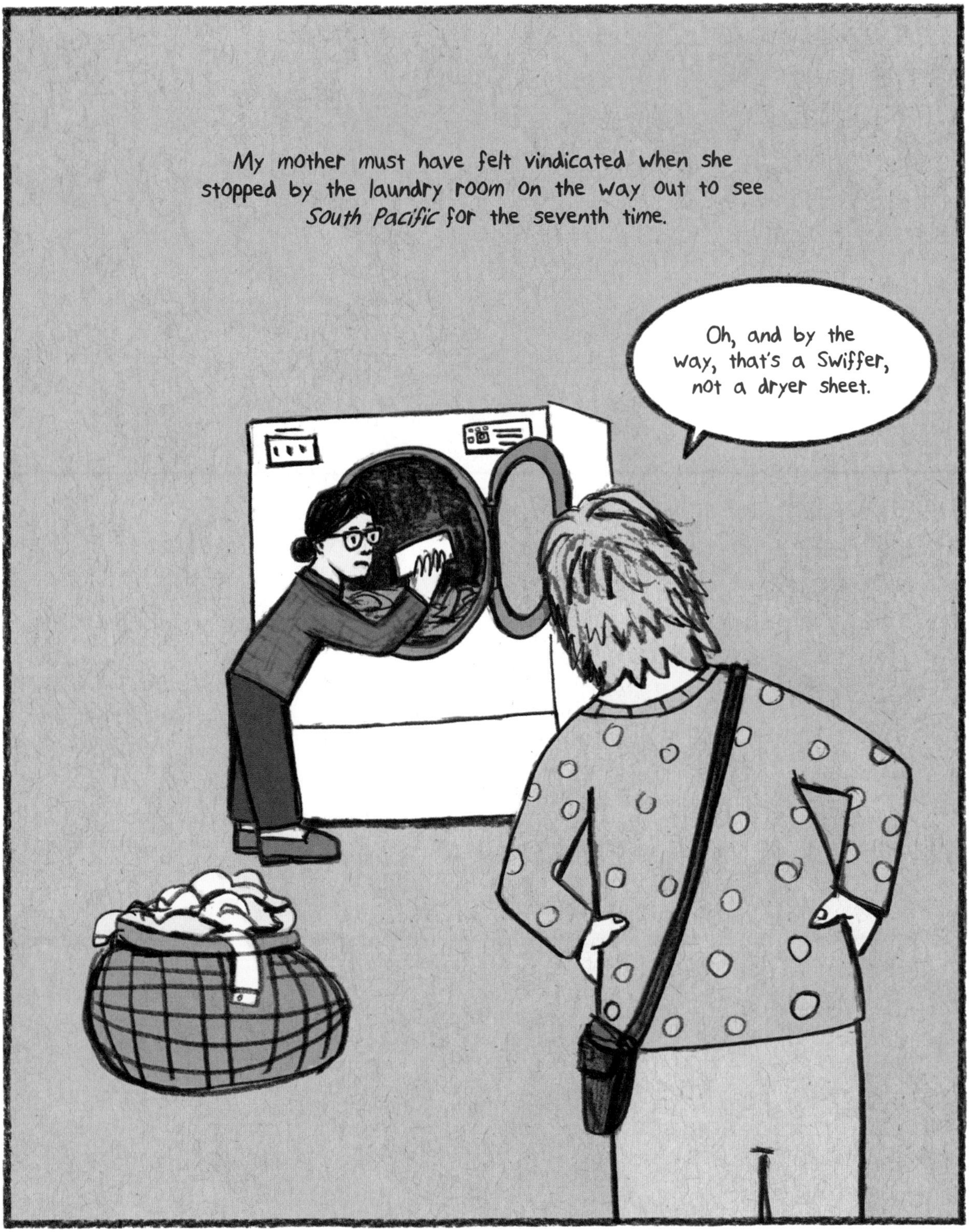
My mother must have felt vindicated when she stopped by the laundry room on the way out to see *South Pacific* for the seventh time.
Oh, and by the way, that's a Swiffer, not a dryer sheet.

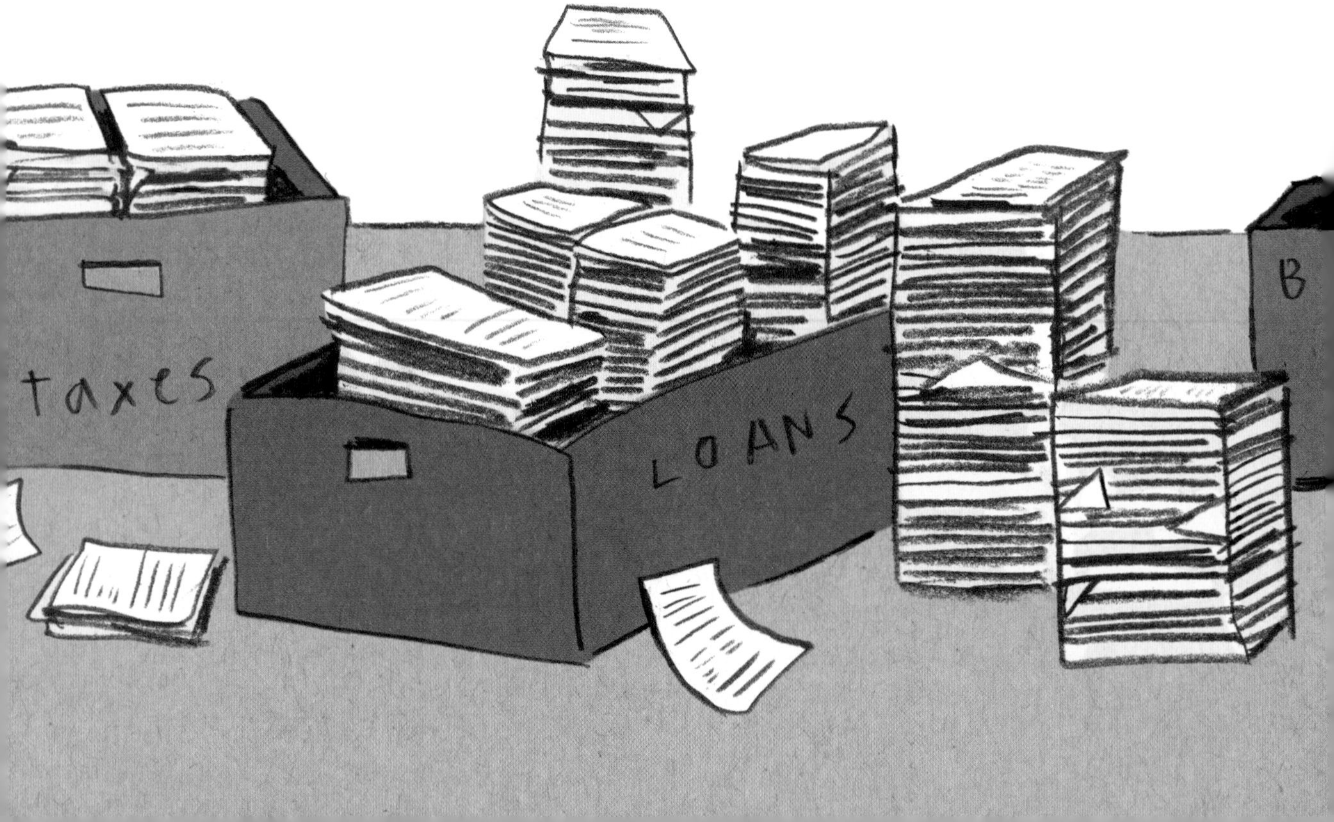
taxes
LOANS
B

Chapter 9

Lost Leaders

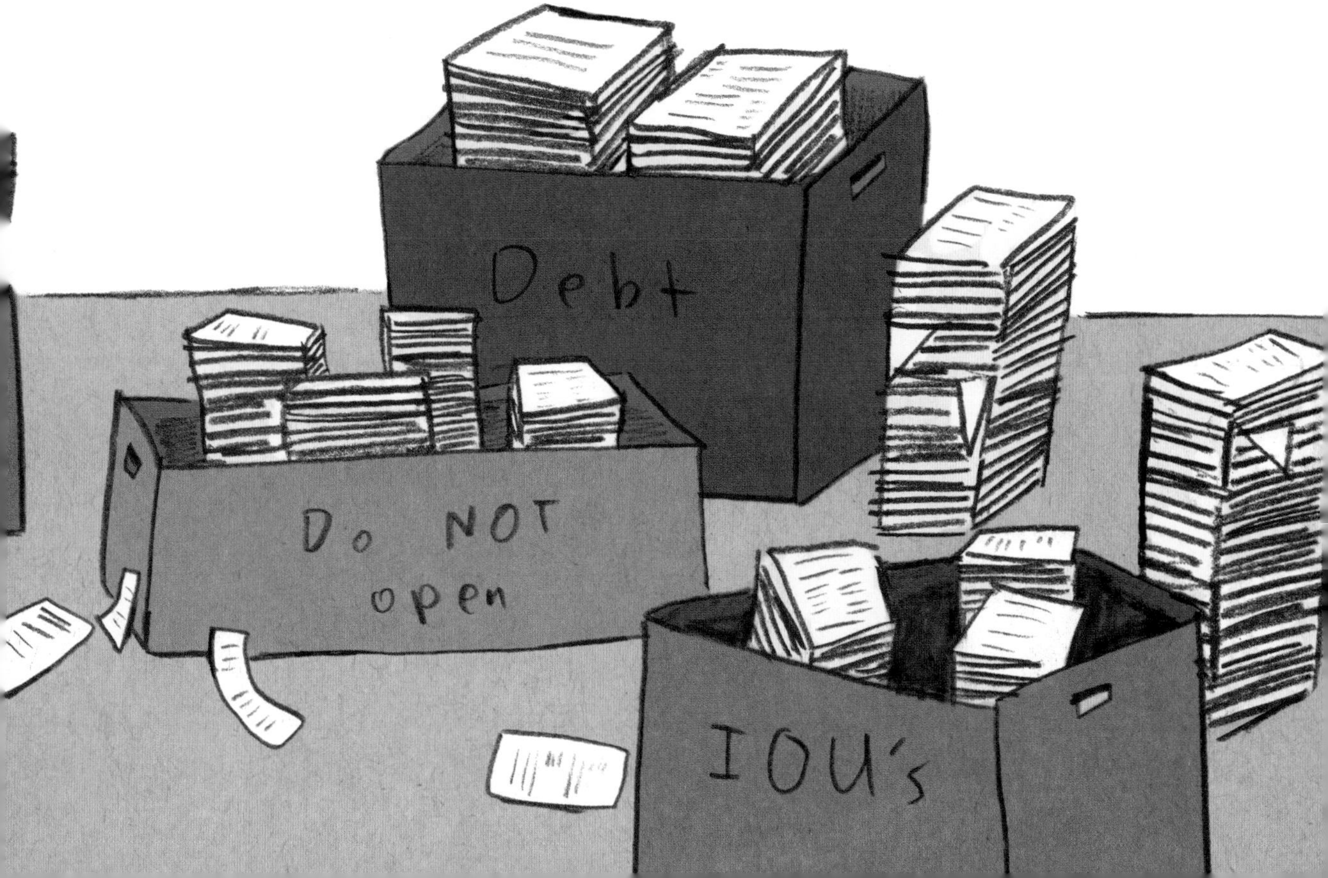
Debt
Do NOT open
IOU's

Opening new stores and making Fishs Eddy bigger would have
been good if the planning, budgeting, and timing had been right,
but all the publicity and success made us feel invincible —
and so we expanded without thinking it through.

With more locations, more staff, and more expenses, it was
official . . . Dave and I were in over our heads in dishes and debt.

We called Dave's mother to borrow money and she said yes, but there would be stipulations.

We were to sign a note that said upon her demise she would be hooked up to every possible method of life support regardless of cost or burden to us. We were to start calling her Mrs. Lenovitz and pay her 25 percent interest if we were even a day late.

But then she winked and gave us a check and said she loved us very much.

Ben and Susie understood what we were going though and tried to be sensitive to our tough financial times.

Marina and I discussed her birthday present, and she said you can just give her twenty dollars in cash and call it a day.

Loans from family weren't enough.

I called vendors to ask for more time on invoices. Dave called landlords to ask for more time on rent.

I called Caroline Kennedy to tell her that Fishs Eddy could no longer be a part of Shop 4 Class, because we were too short on cash to focus on a charity.

Dave and Noah had worked so hard renovating the warehouse on Staten Island, but now our only option was to sell it.

We broke the news gently to Helga, who said it was fine and that she hated the job anyway.

Surprisingly, the warehouse had escalated in value, more than we could ever have imagined.

Dave's instinct to buy the warehouse had saved us. It was enough money to make everything right again, a break that we desperately needed.

Deep inside I agonized over the reality that we may actually have been better at real estate than retail, and Dave confirmed my fears by suggesting we consider doing something other than dishes.

"We've been through so much, maybe we should make up for lost family time and go on family vacations or learn to make chicken that's cooked all the way through. Or maybe even move to Florida."

But I didn't want to stop doing dishes, and I did not want to move to Florida!

Everyone knew Fishs Eddy. After so many years, so many dedicated people, so many window displays and new patterns and magazine articles and the challenging ups and downs of retail, Fishs Eddy had become a real brand. Employees relied on us and customers came from all over to visit us.

I still loved doing dishes and couldn't understand why or how Dave could even think of doing anything else.

One night I had a nightmare.

Dave was with a group of older men on a golf course at a country club in Florida. Dave was wearing a tracksuit and talking with the men about their handicaps and their cholesterol medications and how the latest trend was to have a bar mitzvah at eighty years old.

In the nightmare the scene changed to a casino on a day cruise from Ft. Lauderdale. The room was dark and ominous, except for three people seated with their backs to me. One of them turned around to summon me over.

It was Dave! He was sitting with my mother and Phylma and they were all laughing wickedly and playing the slot machines with loud bells and flashing lights!

Dave and I spent the rest of the night arguing and debating and talking.

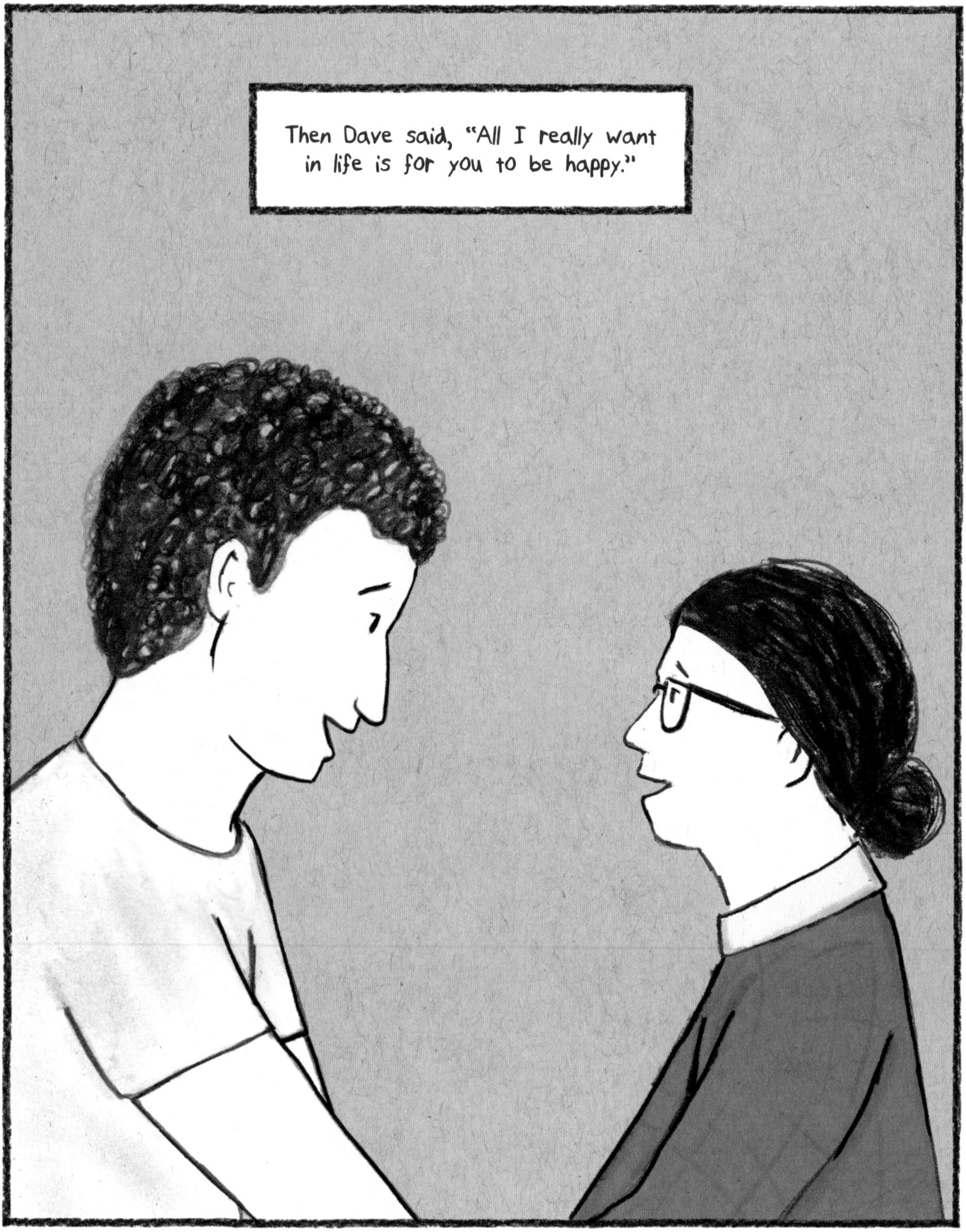
Then Dave said, "All I really want in life is for you to be happy."

The money from the sale of the warehouse was enough to pay off all our debts and hire a CEO who could budget and plan and do all the things that were necessary to do dishes, the right way.

So that's what we did.

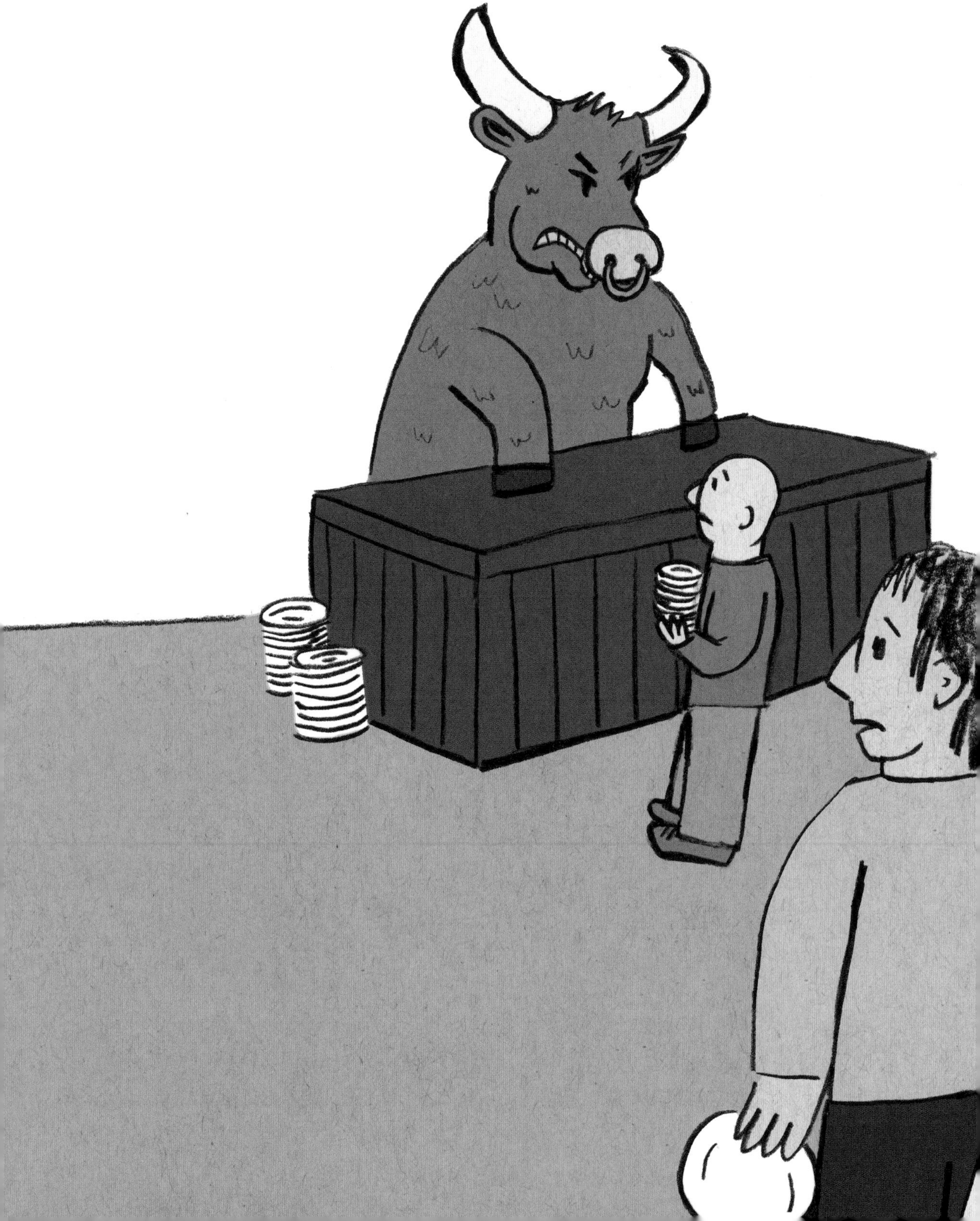

Chapter 10

Bully in a China Shop

Even though he was the first person to answer our ad for a CEO, Carl seemed perfect. His expertise was turning smaller businesses into bigger businesses.

We called a staff meeting to announce that we were entering a new chapter of growth at Fishs Eddy and Carl was here to guide us.

We would have to pay Carl a larger salary than what Dave, Noah, or I made, but we were prepared to make sacrifices for a real professional.

Another sacrifice was that Carl would be working remotely every Friday because he had a country house in Rhode Island with two donkeys, Rubin and Gary, and he liked to spend time with them.

Carl also needed a corporate
credit card to take "people of potential"
on business lunches. The lunches were usually down
the street from the store at the Bluewater Grill.

Carl liked their colossal shrimp cocktail on crushed ice.

One day when Noah walked to the Union Square
farmers' market, he saw Carl sitting outside eating
colossal shrimp cocktails with his donkey breeder.

Carl's donkey breeder wasn't a person with potential to do anything for Fishs Eddy, so we said goodbye to Carl and placed another ad. Felicia appeared to be a better fit, and I thought that we probably should have considered a woman all along.

The staff was confused at the meeting we called to announce Felicia's arrival because we forgot to tell them Carl had left.

Felicia said that gift baskets and staff morale were the two key ingredients to expanding any company.

The first thing Felicia did for staff morale was to award a bonus to whoever sold the most each week. I suggested giving Fishs Eddy gift certificates, but Felicia said she'd conducted an in-depth survey and that the staff preferred cash.

As luck would have it, Felicia won the first week of the competition.

For the gift basket business, Felicia set up an assembly line in the basement that started with a very large empty wicker basket and ended with a hundred-pound shrink-wrapped package, including but not limited to a set of eight dinner plates, eight glasses, eight bowls, eight mugs, eight side plates, a serving platter, a serving bowl, and a box of chocolates for a personal touch.

Felicia did a trial run, sending two of the gift baskets to her home.

She never received the gift baskets, but Felicia did receive notes from both UPS and Federal Express explaining that she would need to find a specialized freight carrier that could handle the weight of the basket and the fragility of the shrink-wrap.

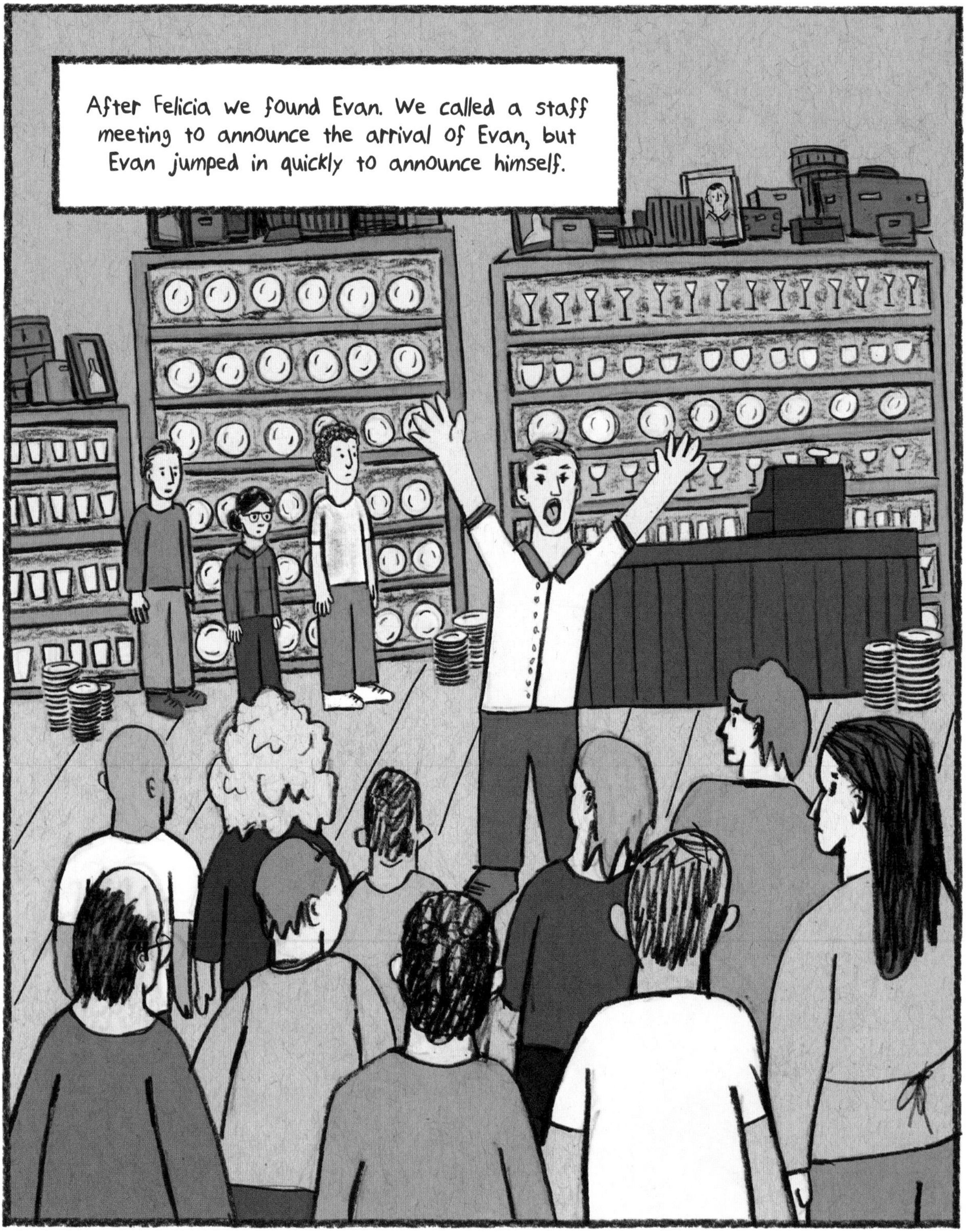
After Felicia we found Evan. We called a staff meeting to announce the arrival of Evan, but Evan jumped in quickly to announce himself.

Evan showed us a lot of analytical spreadsheets to prove that we needed to close every store except our store near Union Square.

He told me that when I saw FOR RENT signs in windows I needed to look down and keep on walking.

I put so much into every store we opened. Closing them was hard. I felt so defeated.

All I could do to feel better was hang the giant map with hundreds of push pins that Dave had rescued years ago from a defunct factory in our corner window under a sign that read FISHS EDDY EXPANSION PLAN.

Because in my mind, we were only shrinking to get bigger.

Evan held weekly meetings with the staff and introduced a budget so that we would start buying merchandise responsibly.

It was an inventory management system commonly used by retailers called an open-to-buy.

Evan told Dave, Noah, and me our problem was that we were always "open-to-buy."

Evan found a new warehouse in Jersey City.

He instructed us to stop calling it a warehouse and start referring to it as a "distribution center," which sounded too professional, considering we had already cluttered the new "distribution center" with our personal stuff.

All of the changes Evan implemented were positive, and for the first time in a long time sales were up. I was so happy to be back on the right track, and so was Dave.

We knew we would soon be a thriving business if we were willing to follow Evan's new way of working, which included lots and lots of meetings. We even had meetings about how we should be meeting more.

Evan's meetings were extra long, so Dave often set the alarm on his phone to ring in the middle of Evan's monologue.

Sorry, guys, that's my reminder to go feed the meter for the car, since parking tickets aren't budgeted in our open-to-buy.

Most of the time Dave never came back to the meeting.

Evan brought his dog, Jeff, to work every day.

Jeff was extremely faithful to Evan, and extremely suspicious of everyone else. Jeff paced the floor, keeping a close and protective eye when Evan was reprimanding the staff for whatever it was they had done wrong at that moment.

The staff was convinced that Jeff was running reconnaissance for Evan. They were sure that Jeff was bad-mouthing and tattling on employees, because each morning Evan would call out their most recent grievances verbatim.

Woof woof woof Matt woof woof Rose woof!

Woof woof Bryan woof woof!

Sales were up every single day. On the rare occasion when sales were not up Evan was intolerant, even if sales were down because of a blizzard. At a meeting one cold February morning, Evan told the staff that they weren't allowed to blame the fourteen inches of snow, below freezing temperatures, or the governor's call for a state of emergency.

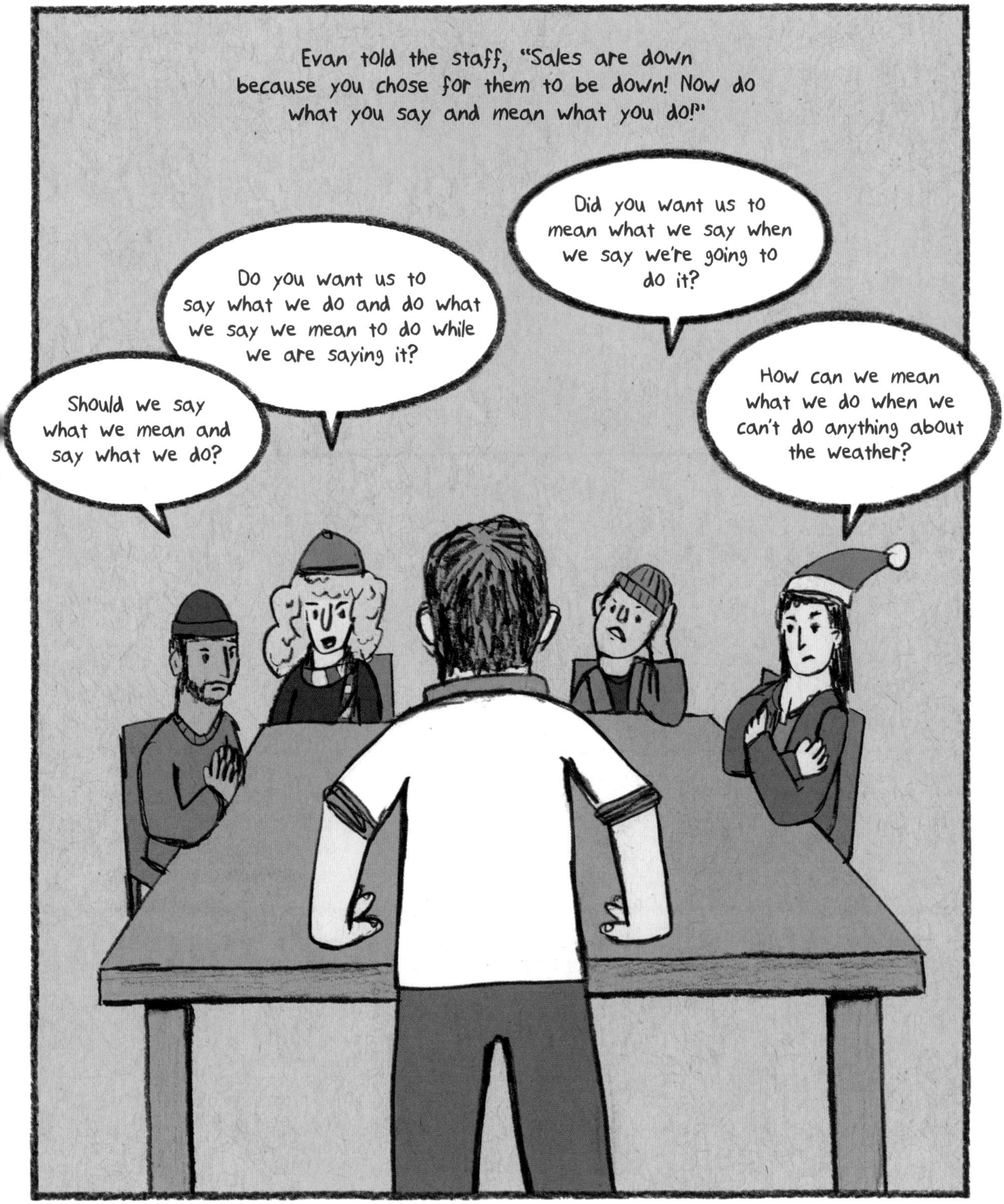
Evan told the staff, "Sales are down because you chose for them to be down! Now do what you say and mean what you do!"
Should we say what we mean and say what we do?
Do you want us to say what we do and do what we say we mean to do while we are saying it?
Did you want us to mean what we say when we say we're going to do it?
How can we mean what we do when we can't do anything about the weather?

After a Monday morning meeting in which Evan made the assistant manager cry, I followed Evan out to the street corner.

I said, "Why were you so demoralizing?" and he said, "I don't have time for this *&@*."

Evan walked away in the middle of the conversation. It was the first time I felt truly small.

When employees confided to Dave and me about their unhappiness, we tried to convince them that Fishs Eddy was finally going to be a Big Business.

We said the proof was in the sales, and if they could just hold on there would be opportunity for everyone.

But then Dave and I took turns complaining to each other. When Dave said that he couldn't take life with Evan much longer, I begged him to have patience and reminded him how we were finally profitable. When I cried about Evan to Dave, he threw my words right back at me.

This is what you wanted, remember?

Dave believed we had missed our opportunity to start a new chapter in our lives.

We started to argue all the time.

It seemed as though the more we fought and the more miserable we became, the higher sales climbed.

Just when things couldn't get any worse,
Dave lost the one person who never
believed in him — his mother.

Dave started to smoke pot more than usual.

For his birthday Ben and Susie bought their dad a new pipe at their favorite smoke shop, but even that didn't cheer him up.

I started getting unfamiliar feelings, a numbness in my fingers and heaviness in my legs. When I called my mother to tell her, she said I was under too much pressure at Fishs Eddy.

My mother said I should take a break and come visit her in Boca because she'd just bought her burial plot — a package deal including five years of free membership at the synagogue, plus two free Shabbat dinners.

My mother was excited that Phylma got the same package.

Dave said, "Hmmm. I guess the burial plot store felt pretty safe offering five years of free membership."

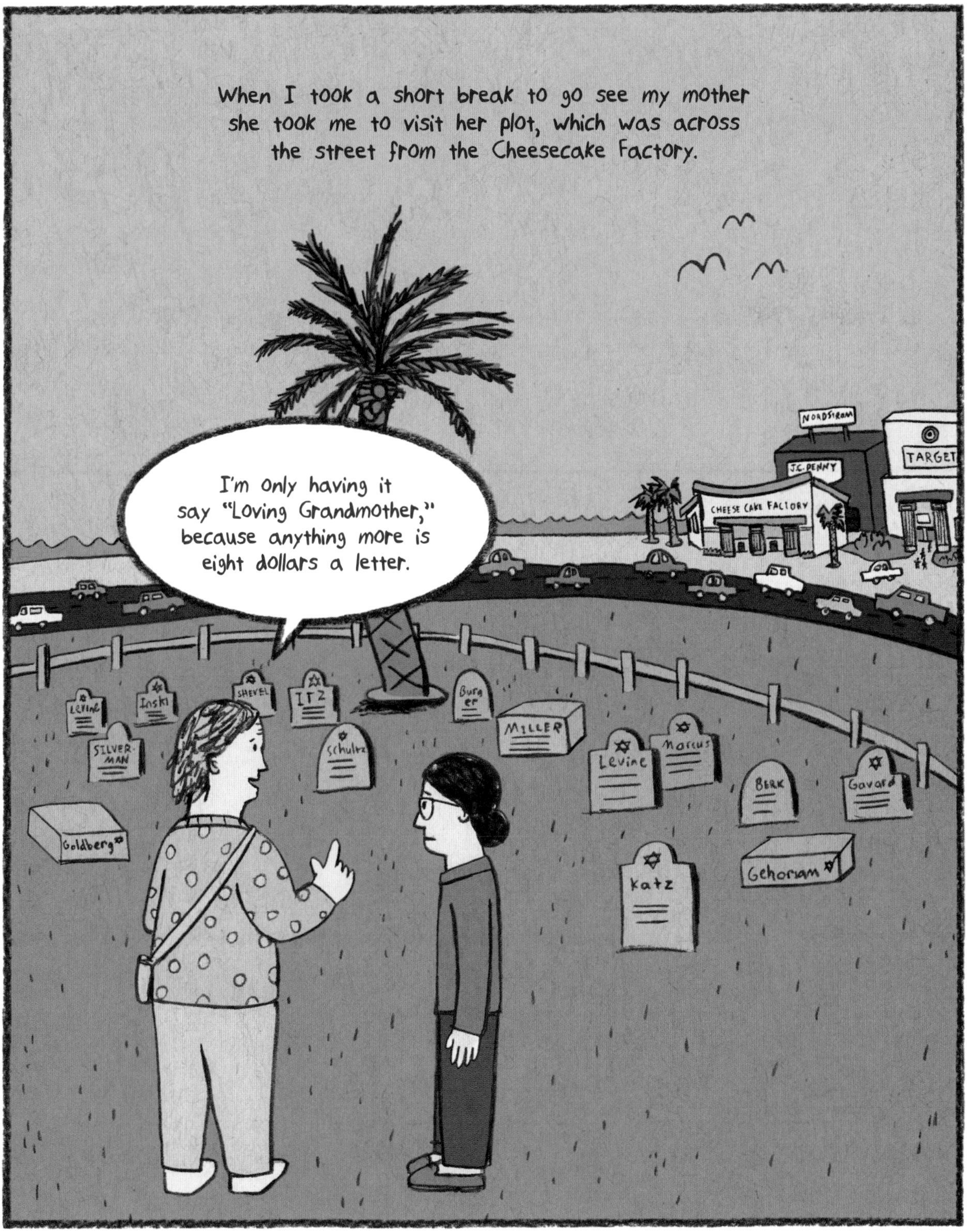
When I took a short break to go see my mother she took me to visit her plot, which was across the street from the Cheesecake Factory.
I'm only having it say "Loving Grandmother," because anything more is eight dollars a letter.
NORDSTROM
TARGET
J.C. PENNY
CHEESE CAKE FACTORY
MILLER
Levine
Marcus
BERK
Goldberg
Katz
SILVER-MAN
Schultz

My sister Ilene and I talked about how organized our mother was about everything.

We'll have to sit shivah for an entire week, but the good news is Mommy prepaid for it all.

Is it rude to ask if she covered the catering?

134

I desperately needed something to take my mind off Evan, so when I passed a sign outside a bar that read OPEN MIC NIGHT, TRY YOUR HAND AT COMEDY, I went in.

I told funny stories about Dave, Ben, and Susie and got a few laughs from the audience.

I started going to open mic nights often, thinking I had found the perfect outlet to forget about Evan.

My mother called to say, "Honey, I'm coming to town and I'd like to see one of those little comedy thingies you do."

I told my mother that I'd stopped — at the audience's request.

Which wasn't far from the truth.

EXIT

After a few performances it was clear that I was not meant to be on a stage.

I was meant to be in a store, doing what I loved most — dishes.

On parents' night, Dave and I went to hear Susie's principal give a lecture. It was about bullying.

The principal said, "You don't have to hit someone to bully them and cause emotional harm." She said, "It's crucial to remove the bully from the situation before more damage is done."

We were silent the whole way home.

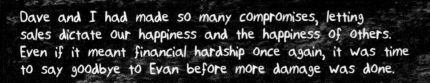

Dave and I had made so many compromises, letting sales dictate our happiness and the happiness of others. Even if it meant financial hardship once again, it was time to say goodbye to Evan before more damage was done.

In the middle of the night, the ghost of Dave's mother came to both of us with words of wisdom.

Whatever happens in life, you two need to stick together . . . because who else would have either one of you!?

I hated firing people, so that task was usually left to Dave.

The only person I ever fired, years ago, showed up the next morning and told me I was just having a bad day.

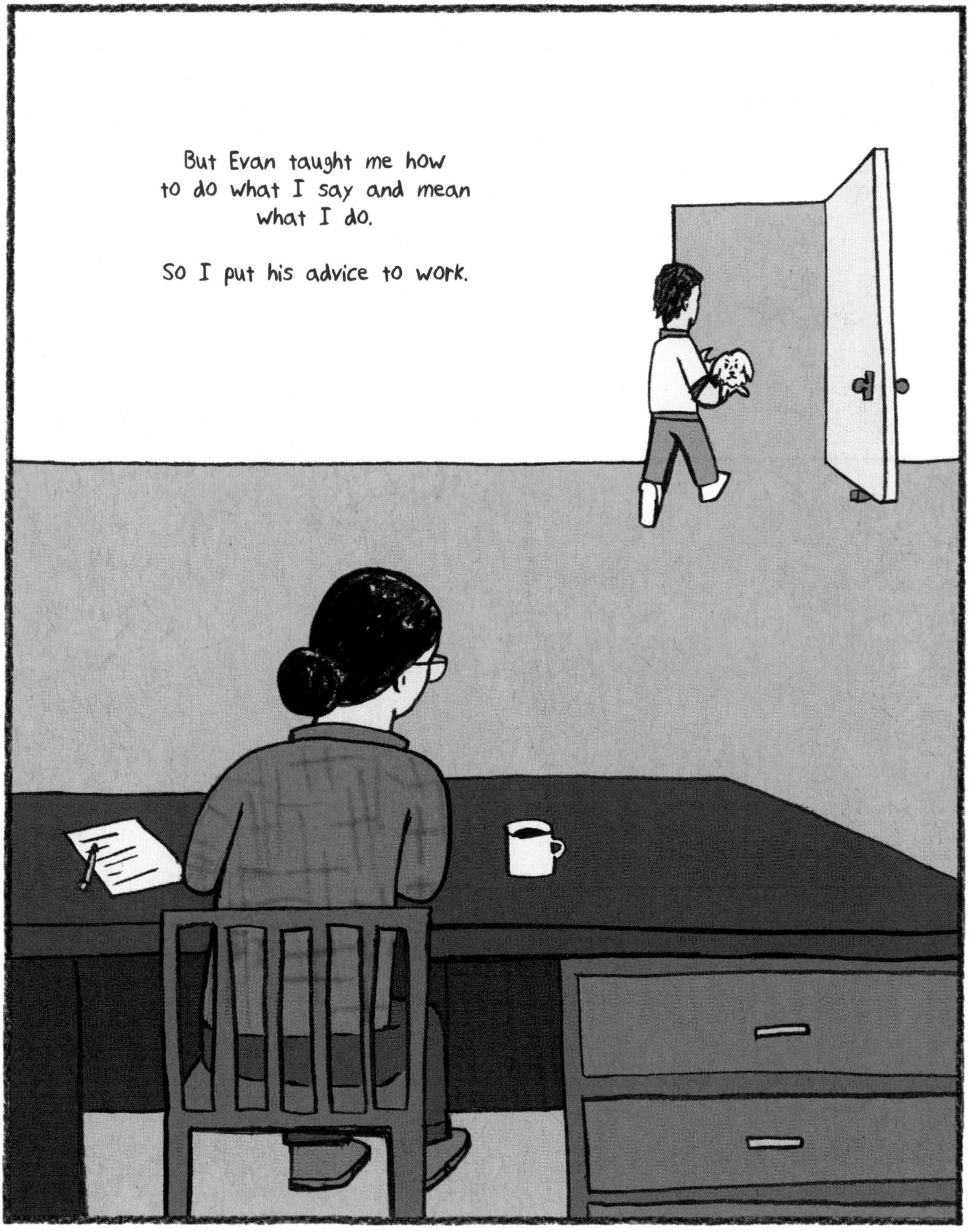
But Evan taught me how to do what I say and mean what I do.
So I put his advice to work.

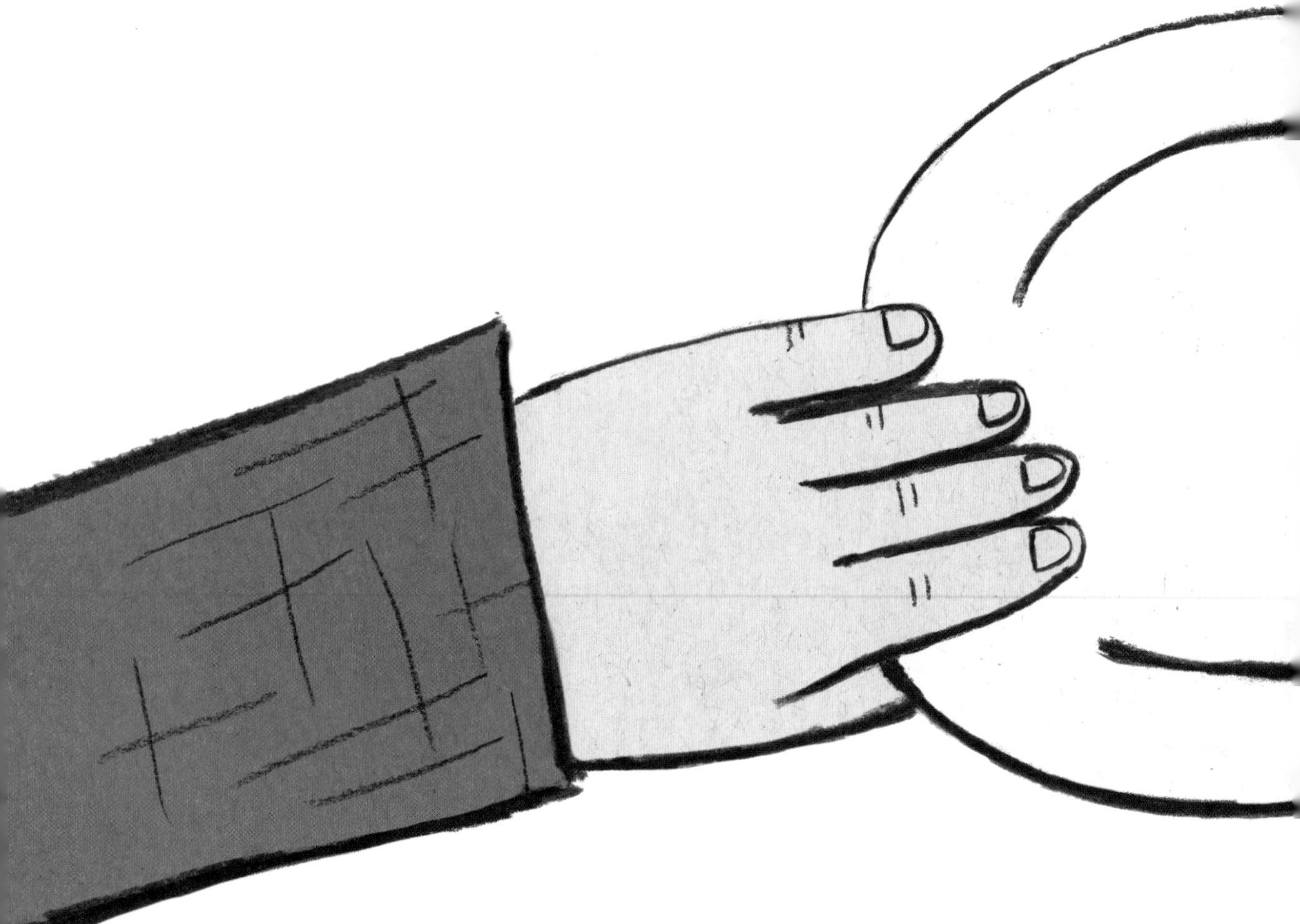

Chapter 11

Dishing It Out

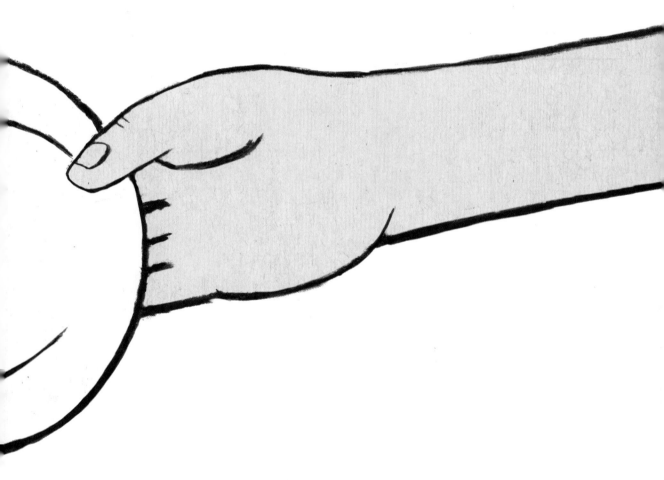

Evan was gone, but the *numbness* and heaviness in my legs was still there.

Sometimes it felt as though I was walking through wet cement, and sometimes my balance was so off that I had to hold on to Dave.

Neurologists in lab coats announced that the *symptoms* that had been brewing over the past few years meant I had multiple sclerosis.

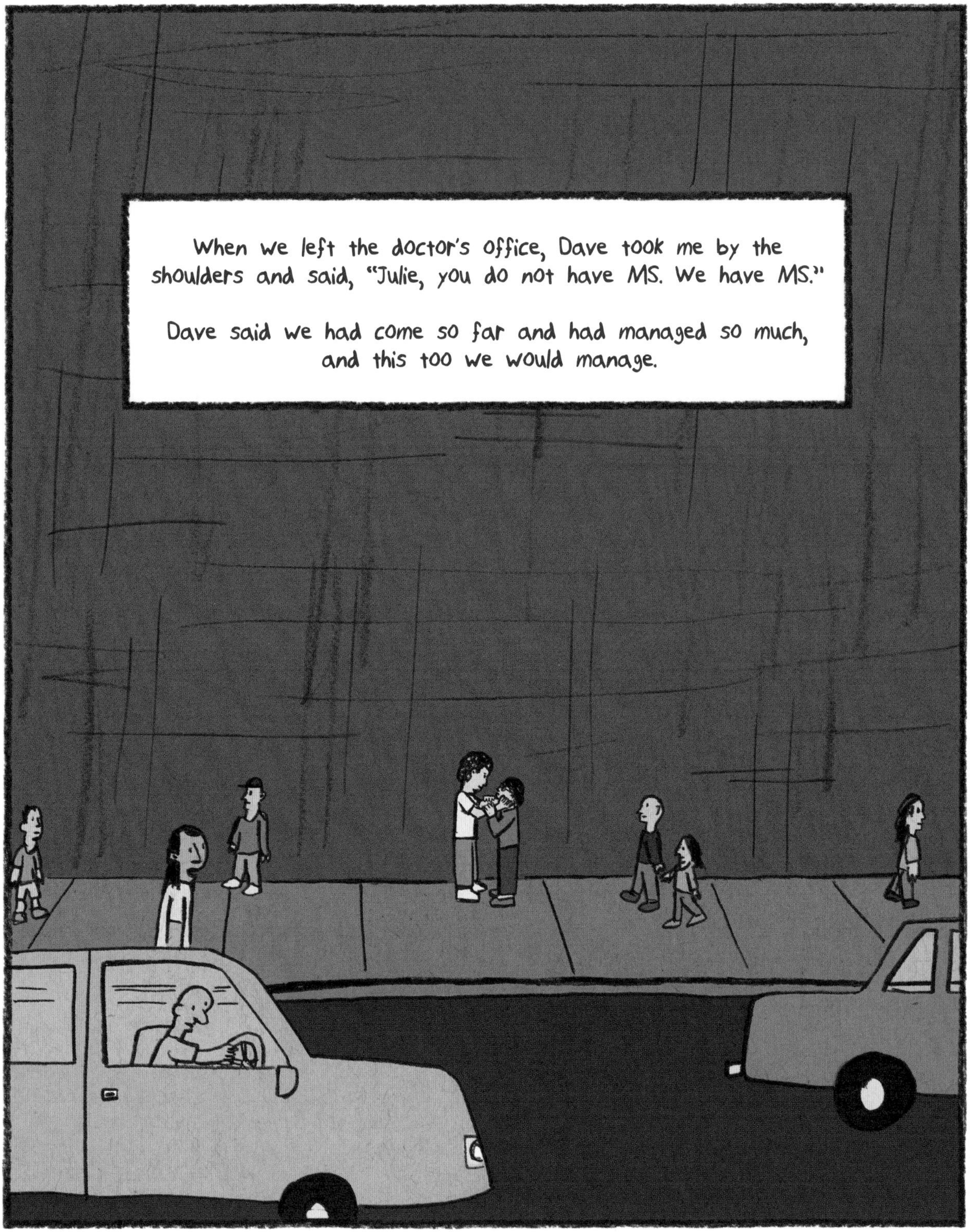
When we left the doctor's office, Dave took me by the shoulders and said, "Julie, you do not have MS. We have MS."
Dave said we had come so far and had managed so much, and this too we would manage.

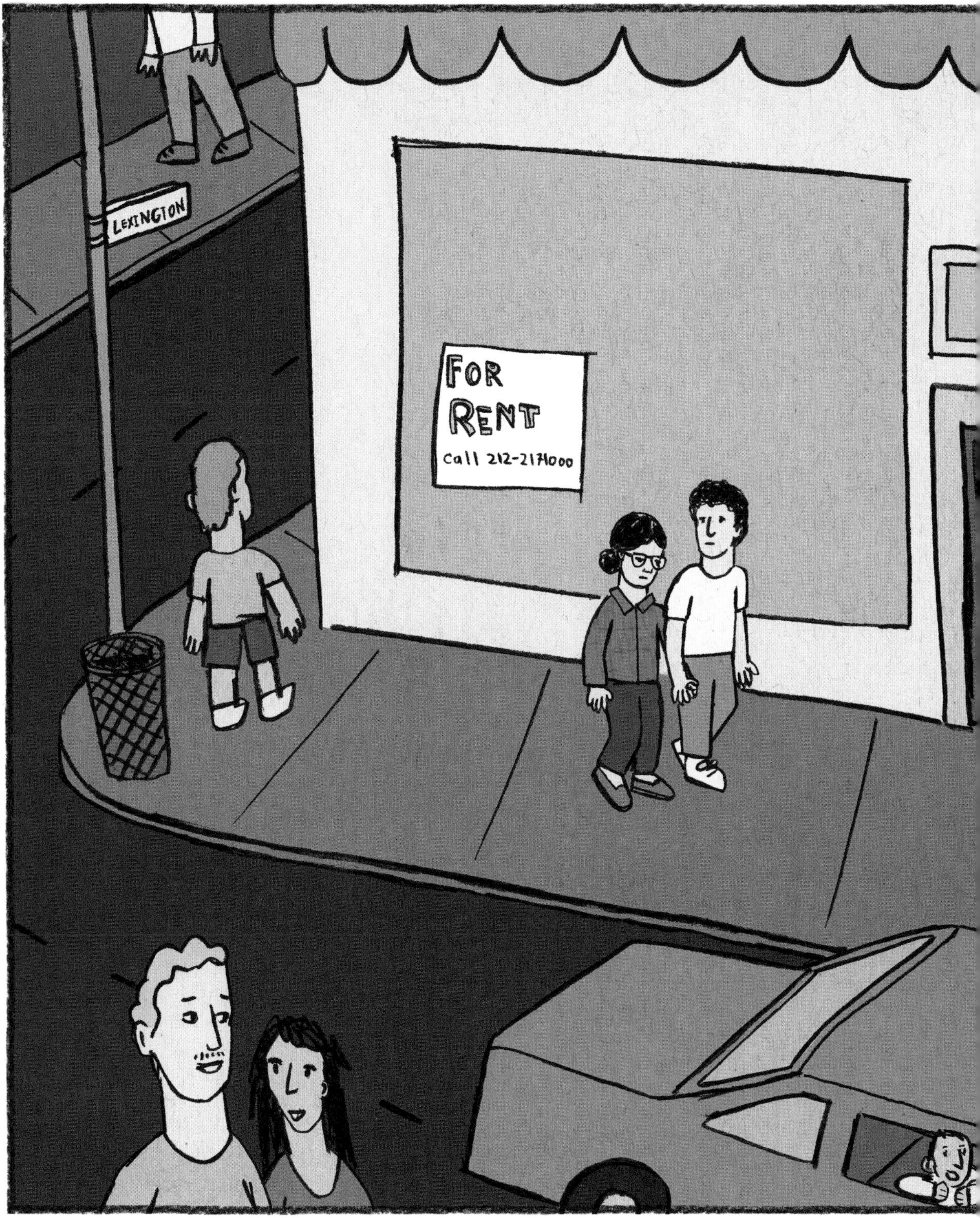
LEXINGTON
FOR RENT
call 212-2171000

We walked home from the doctor's and passed a lot of FOR RENT signs in empty store windows, but now they weren't important to me.

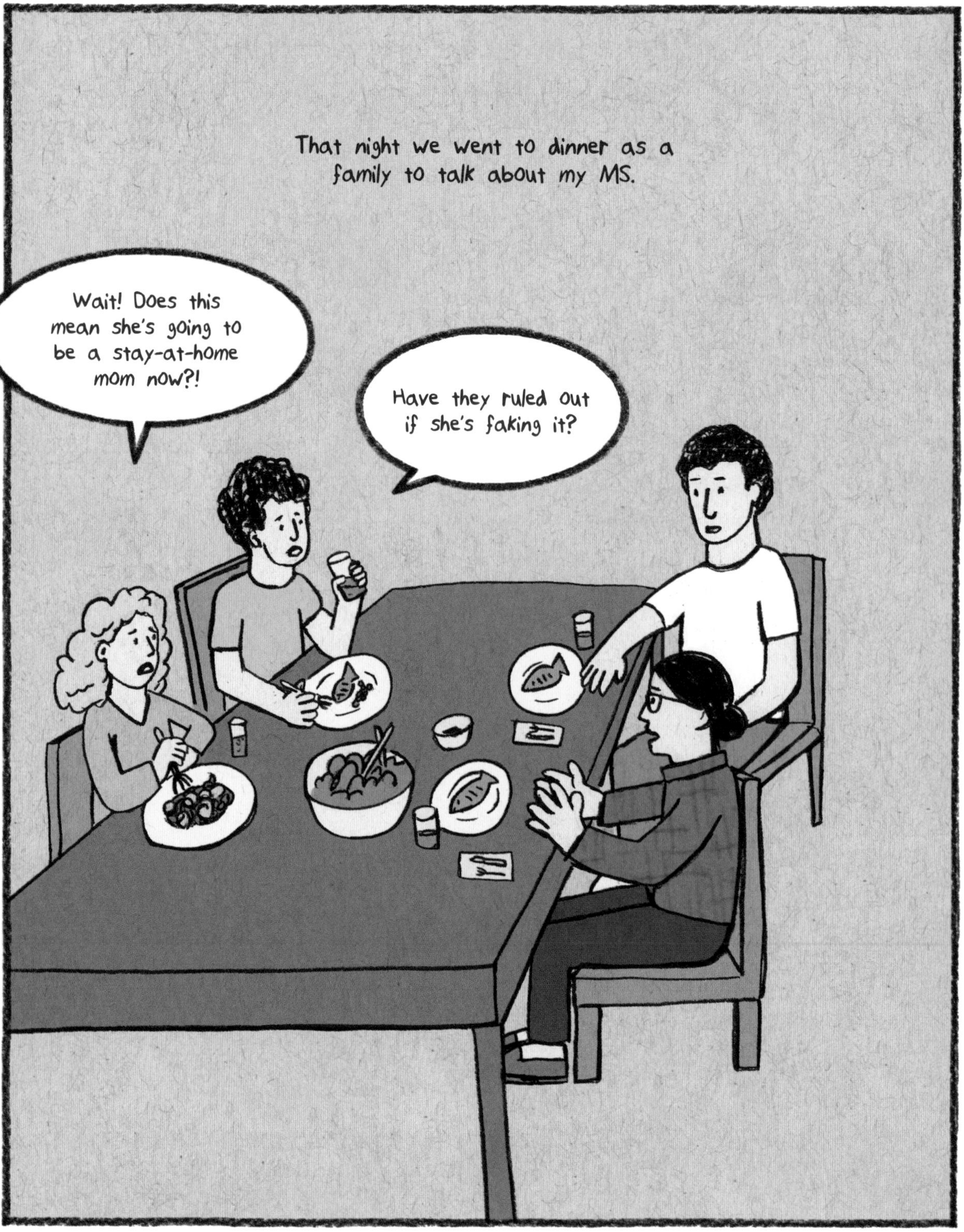
That night we went to dinner as a family to talk about my MS.
Wait! Does this mean she's going to be a stay-at-home mom now?!
Have they ruled out if she's faking it?

Dave, Noah, and I were determined to hold on to everything Evan had implemented that was productive and say goodbye to everything that had caused so much upheaval.

While we braced ourselves for the worst, sales continued to climb.

Fewer meetings meant more time to design new patterns, collaborate with new artists, and be creative once again, which was exactly what I wanted to do.

I messengered a letter to the designer Todd Oldham asking if he would consider creating dishware for Fishs Eddy.

When Todd called soon after receiving the letter I made sure not to tell him to shut up, like I had done with Caroline Kennedy.

BIRD

CAT

FISH

I remembered that sometimes when people believe in you, they really do call you back.

And I remembered again how much I loved doing dishes.

We also made more time for family trips. On our Arizona vacation, Dave, Ben, Susie, and I were running to the gate to catch our plane.

When Susie noticed that I was way ahead, she hollered, "Mom's MS is BS!"

Wait for us!

Then we all stopped for a second because we were laughing too hard to run. I was still first to the gate.

Dave saw an opportunity to expand when an adjacent space behind the Broadway store came up for sale.

Once again, Dave convinced the Small Business Administration to help us buy it.

This time we knew to grow in just one location.

I reminded Dave that we had learned so many lessons, and Dave said, "We should be certified geniuses by now."

On our twenty-fifth wedding anniversary, Dave and I decided to do a "life walk" and visit all the places in the city that were part of our history.

We started on the corner of 15th Street and 6th Avenue, because that was the location of the little glassware shop where I first met Dave.

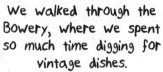

We walked through the Bowery, where we spent so much time digging for vintage dishes.

We went by the Sunshine Diner where we drew the Skyline pattern on a napkin, and we stopped at a Starbucks on 3rd Avenue and 21st, formerly Weinstock Brothers Hardware.

We walked all the way up to the corner of 77th and Broadway, where many years ago I had spotted a FOR RENT sign in the window and convinced Dave to open another location.

And then back down to the corner store at Mercer and Broome, where I had spotted yet another FOR RENT sign, and we'd opened another store.

We made our way west to Hudson Street and then walked two blocks up to the White Horse Tavern, where Dylan Thomas used to drink beer and write poetry, and where Dave and I used to go after work for hamburgers with Cecil and Milton.

We walked through the playground in Union Square, where we used to take Ben and Susie, and we walked through the now beautiful Union Square Park, which had become a model for other business improvement districts in New York City.

We remembered our mothers' sound advice . . .

Union Square will never amount to anything.

We walked down to Ground Zero, where there's
a new World Trade Center and a gift shop that
sells our New York City Skyline dishes.

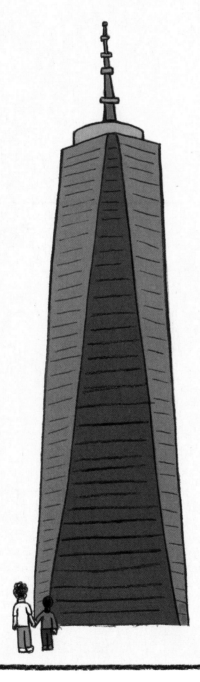

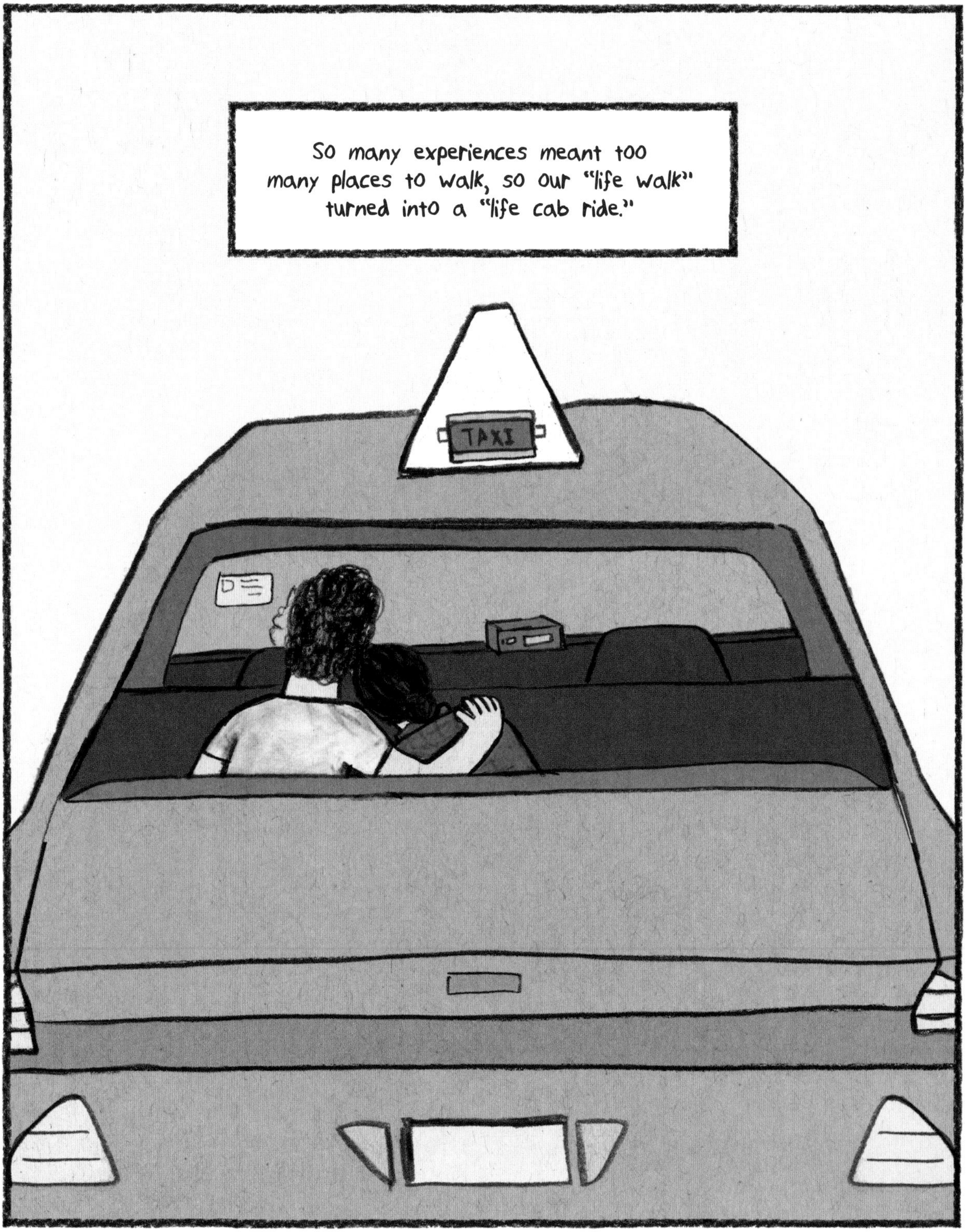
So many experiences meant too many places to walk, so our "life walk" turned into a "life cab ride."
TAXI

Dave and I didn't even make it to half the places we wanted to go because it was getting late and we were getting tired and we had to get home to the kids . . . to order Chinese takeout.

Epilogue

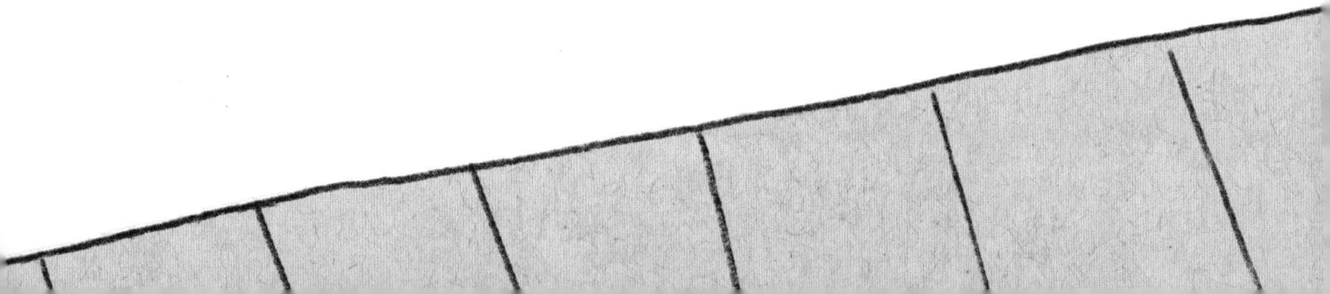

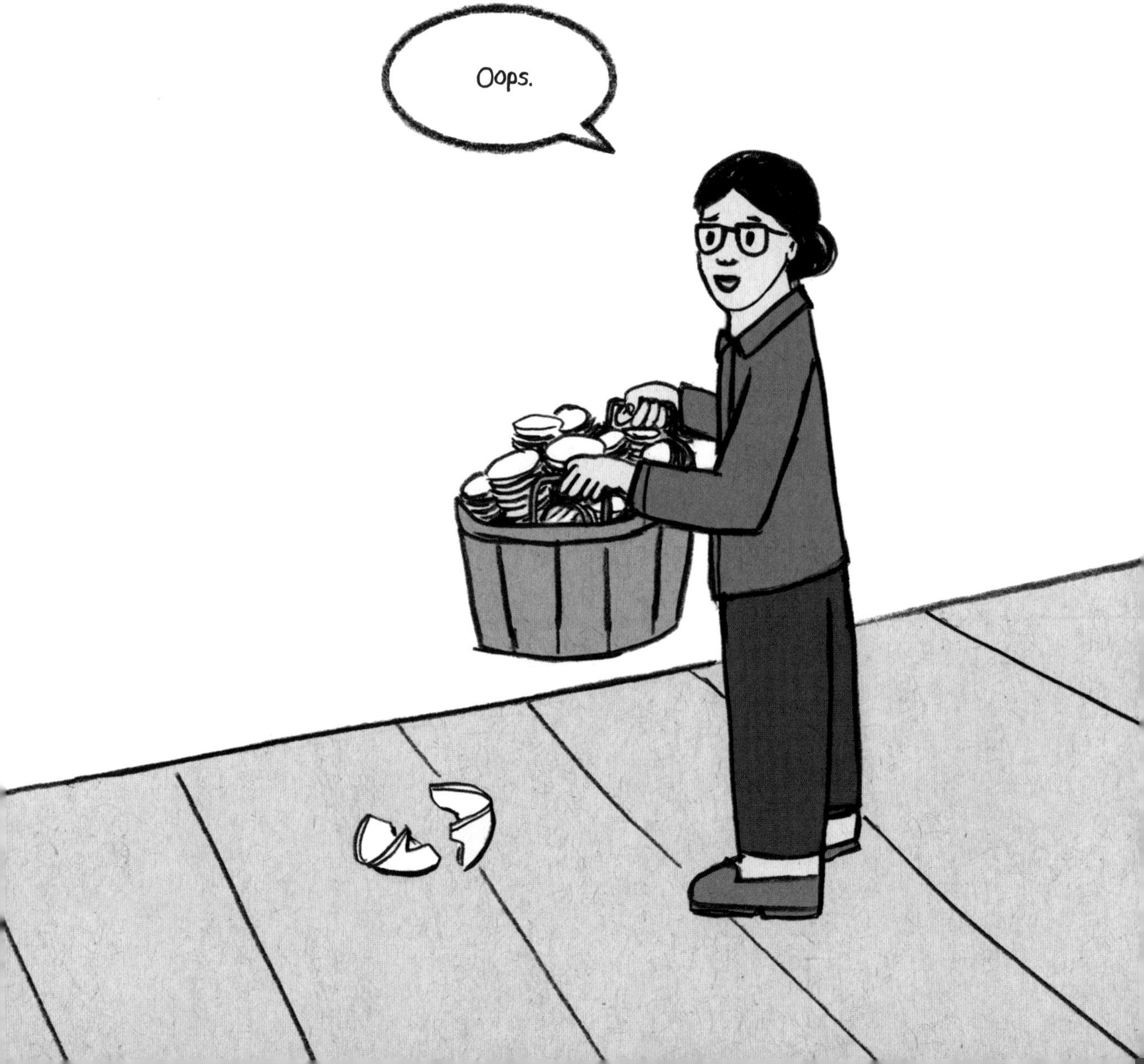
Oops.

Acknowledgments

Thank you to my editor, Amy Gash,
and publisher, Elisabeth Scharlatt, at Algonquin
for supporting me in more ways than just this book.

To the art department at Algonquin for all the back and forths.

To Rose Wong for doing the brilliant color and design of
this book, for making it gorgeous, elegant, and way beyond words!

To my agents, Alison Fargis and Ellen Scordato at Stonesong, for believing in me.

To Amanda Chung and Christopher Lucero for doing anything
and everything to make this book happen.

To Joey Cavalieri for putting us on the right track and guiding us.

To Nancy Kelton for teaching me to "get out of my own way" and write.

Thank you to Peter Kranes and Noah Lenovitz, my partners,
my friends, my brothers, and my support system every single day.

To Lisa Lenovitz and Bruce Eaton for their unconditional love
and too many other things to name.

To Stan and Jon for being my friends, support, and sounding board.

To Alyson and Wendy, who I couldn't live without!

To Jon Burden, my mentor since forever.

To Matte O'Brien for organizing my world,
all while laughing and singing show tunes.

To Todd Oldham and Tony Longoria for your friendship and love.

Thank you to Robin Einbinder and the MS Society for helping so many people, like me.

To my dad for inspiring me from the first day we met!

To my mother for being everything to me . . . and allowing me to talk smack.

To Ilene and Dena . . . because sisters still rule.

Thank you to Team Fishs Eddy for the privilege of doing dishes with you, every day!

And most of all, thank you to Ben and Susie for spending all my money,
giving me gray hairs, making endless fun of me . . . and giving me a
reason to wake up each morning. Keep up the good work!

JULIE GAINES grew up in Staten Island and studied painting at Syracuse University. After college she moved to Manhattan, where she met Dave Lenovitz. Together, they opened Fishs Eddy. Thirty years later, Julie's favorite pastime is still doing dishes.

The son of Fishs Eddy co-founders, BEN LENOVITZ was born and raised in New York City. He studied painting at SUNY New Paltz and now lives in Brooklyn, where he has built his business called Art on Block.